Saying *yes!*

Conversations on a World that Works for All

Edited by Sarah Ruth van Gelder
from *YES! A Journal of Positive Futures*

The Postitive Futures Network

is an independant, nonprofit

organization that supports people's

active engagement in creating

a more just, sustainable, and

compassionate world.

Cover Illustration © Michael Woloschinow

Funding for this publication has been provided by a
grant from the New Visions Foundation.

Printed on recycled paper.

Printed in Canada

Contents

Introduction

> "Until one is committed, there is hesitancy, the chance to draw back. ... Whatever you can do or dream you can, begin it. Boldness has genius, power and magic in it. Begin it now."
> — *Goethe*

In the four years I've been editing *YES!* magazine, I've often found myself in despair. I research the trends in climate disruption and witness our cavalier destruction of fragile ecosystems. I hear the story of women who discover their breast milk is loaded with toxins as a result of the widespread use of agricultural and industrial chemicals – and then learn about the children whose development is jeopardized by their exposure in the womb. I learn that the country that most prides itself on freedom and tolerance imprisons at a higher rate than nearly any other country in the world, and hear stories of the solitary confinement, brutality, and rape experienced by the women, men, and young people behind bars.

I first became aware that there was something very wrong when I spent a year in India with my family as an eight-year-old child. I learned about a country with ancient roots and wisdom, art, music, temples, dance. I also saw countless children going hungry, begging for subsistence. Later, I was appalled to hear stories coming out of Vietnam, Chile, and Central America — stories of US government complicity, and in some cases leadership, in gross human rights violations and exploitation. I gradually became aware that while our own history is full of both the heroism and innovation described in my school textbooks, our prosperity is also built on the labor of African-born slaves and their descendents and on the lands, and in many cases the know-how, of the native peoples of North America.

How does someone filled with stories and images of despair edit a publication named *YES!*? Fortunately for me, for every story of inhumanity, I also encountered a story of courage and compassion. Through my family's Quaker affiliation and through various activist circles, I met people who think deeply about their lives and their effects on the world and who act based on their values. I have been blessed with some powerful teachers, some of whom appear in these pages.

Meeting these people and seeing the innovations they have introduced gave me hope. But I also wanted to understand the causes of our persistent problems. I came to see that the deep dysfunctions of our society are grounded in a debilitating worldview that is as much in evidence in capitalist societies as in communist societies. That worldview, often referred to as modernism, values economic growth, domination, technological progress, materialism, and a reductionist approach to knowledge (that is, a belief that all knowledge can be derived from dissecting parts rather than from comprehending wholes).

Of course modernism has made some enormously important contributions to human progress:

• It gave us modern medicine and the elimination of any number of diseases along with the technology that could free us from poverty and drudgery – should we choose to use it that way.

• It provided the foundation for the concept of individual human rights and freedom, from the emancipation of slaves to the more contemporary efforts to recognize the rights of women, workers, children, gays and lesbians, people of all colors, genders, and religions.

• It gave us the freedom to pursue truth and knowledge even when that inquiry took us outside the orthodoxies of the church or the wealthy and powerful – what a liberation from the era of the Inquisition and witch burnings!

But the success of modernism created a whole new set of problems. It created the conditions for new, powerful empires of monumental size and power to exploit and oppress people, and eventually to wreak environmental devastation. Poverty multiplied as the wealth of a select few grew. Wars were fought to protect the interests of these empires. And the expansion of science and technological know-*how* did not include either the know *why* or the know *whether*. The development of our capacity for ethics, beauty, love, spirituality, transcendence, wisdom is lost in the mad race to accumulate power and wealth. The natural world is sold at fire-sale prices to expedite the massive economic and military buildup.

Now we are facing the consequences, and the world's scientists have warned us that there isn't much time. Worldwatch Institute estimates that 11 percent of the world's bird species, 25 percent of mammal species, and 34 percent of fish species are vulnerable or in immediate danger of extinction. Global warming is undermining the delicate balance of precipitation, soil, microorganisms, and climate stability that makes agriculture reliable. While there is much celebration of the booming economy, at least in the US, the top 1 percent saw their income rise more than 80 percent from 1979 to 1994, but the 60 percent at the bottom saw a *decline* in income. Worldwide, the richest 450 people now control more of the world's resources than half the world's population.

We are at a choice point now that is unlike those faced by previous generations. We must reorient society around values that will allow a sustainable way of life or face a worldwide ecological and social crisis.

Fortunately for all of us, there are literally millions of people across the world involved in this creative search for the parameters of a new society. Some are protecting forests, organizing community gardens, redesigning neighborhoods and cities, building compassionate and effective organizations, developing theories of economics that take nature into account, organizing opposition to the World Trade Organization and other promoters of corporate globalization. Many are searching for ways to heal themselves, their families, and their communities from the effects of environmental and social toxins. Others are rediscovering ancient wisdom or searching for sources of meaning when the sirens' call of money and consumerism fails to deliver happiness.

At *YES!* magazine, we explore these nascent experiments and the growing social and consciousness movements built on people's yearning for a just, sustainable, and compassionate future. But beyond that, we look for signs of a society emerging that is built on this new worldview and this new sense of possibility. One powerful sign can be found in the research of Paul Ray and Sherry Anderson. They suggest that a growing number of people, whom they dub Cultural Creatives, shares a constellation of values that differ from those that characterize the modern/industrial age. Environmental awareness is fundamental to this emerging group, along with a deep appreciation of diverse cultures. The characteristics traditionally associated with the feminine (nurturing, network building, personal development) are valued as well as those associated with the masculine, and there is greater concern for family, community, and future generations than for material accumulation. According to Ray and Anderson, the subculture that holds these values now numbers close to 50 million people in the United States alone, making it a group that could exert a major influence over our future. In some arenas this influence is already strong. The rapid growth of the alternative health and healing and organics markets is an indication of the size and strength of this population.

The mainstream media, immersed as it is in the modernist mindset, is only now beginning to recognize the existence of this group. As the media becomes increasingly concentrated in the hands of the most powerful of modernist institutions, the corporation, their understanding of this emerging subculture is likely to remain limited to occasional stories of protests or new "market sectors." With so little evidence in the mainstream media of their values or influence, many Cultural Creatives believe that they are powerless – that they alone, along with a few friends, are developing new values and approaches.

The good news is that, media ignorance notwithstanding, these values have spread far more quickly and more deeply than most of us imagine. There is now the real possibility that we can act together to create a truly sustainable, life-affirming society. If we succeed, future generations will remember us as the ones who made the shift, the ones who chose life over eco-cide, community over alienation, justice and respect over degradation.

But good intentions will not be enough. If we are to make needed changes before destruction to the Earth becomes irreversible, we will have to consciously choose to turn our values and caring into action.

In this book, you'll find people who have made such a choice, and in doing so have become some of the leading visionaries for a more life-sustaining future. While none would claim to carry the whole answer, each is exploring some significant part of the picture: how we might eliminate poverty, how we can reduce the pervasive effect of consumerism on our lives, how businesses can produce without undermining the Earth's life-support capacities, how we can reclaim our future from the grip of global corporations, how we might redesign our cities to foster community and a healthy environment, how we can build understanding between races and reclaim our capacity to heal ourselves and one another.

I am grateful to have had the opportunity to work with each of these people over the past several years as we prepared these interviews for publication in *YES!* magazine. And I am delighted to be sharing these conversations with you – I hope you will find them as inspiring as I have.

Sarah Ruth van Gelder
Executive editor
YES! A Journal of Positive Futures
Bainbridge Island, Washington

Banking on Earth, Light, and Water

Berito Kuwar U'wa is a leader of the U'wa indigenous people of Colombia, who are struggling to maintain their way of life as Occidental Petroleum seeks to exploit oil reserves on their traditional homeland.

Are indigenous ways the ways of the past? Or do they hold lessons for our common future? Berito Kuwar U'wa is calling on us not only to save his people, but to save the Earth.

Sarah van Gelder: Many people in the United States believe that foreign oil companies and the jobs they bring are welcomed. What are your views that?

Berito Kuwar U'Wa: I believe that the U'wa people were born in a world that is older than everything else. We have a traditional *constitution* that comes from many years ago, which is our way of understanding how the world relates to itself – how life works.

The petroleum companies go in with their computers and make decrees; they make their own constitution. Theirs is new. The petroleum companies plant the seeds of their constitution throughout the world. They plant the seeds of their constitution, and it's not for the benefit of those countries, nor for the benefit of those people. That's what we should not permit.

The world was not created for the petroleum companies. Our education teaches us to look at the unity of the world. Their education teaches them that they can make these constitutions, that they can make these laws so that they can be the landlords of the world, so that they control the whole world until it dies. They shouldn't be allowed to do this.

There are two constitutions. The constitution that we have is called "The Constitution of the Earth." The other constitution is called " The Constitution of Money." What's happening is that the Constitution of Mother Earth – the oldest constitution – is being passed over and destroyed by the constitution of the various governments and of the petroleum companies.

Sarah: *Could you explain a bit about how your economy operates based on this Constitution of the Earth rather than the Constitution of Money?*

Berito: We don't need money to build a house, for example. If somebody wants to build a house, they plant a cassava plant. And then they take the cassava and make a drink called "chicha." This "chicha" is like our money, because with that we pay people to come and help build the house.

The real money that we have is the Earth. From the Earth comes everything that we make, everything that we sow, that we grow, that we consume. We don't have to sell things and we don't have to buy things. We say, "The sun is the money," and the Earth is also money. It's our gold. The water is also our gold. These are things that we need to value so that life can continue. We need light because right now we have hunger, we need food, and where does that food come from? It comes from light, it comes from the Earth.

And water. What is water worth? How do you value it? Water should be free for everyone, but now we're supposed to pay the government for water. The water is born in our territory. Water is a benefit for everyone; all the world has property rights over water. If somebody should have to pay for water, they should have to pay the landlord of the world. But really, the government doesn't want to work, they don't want to dirty their hands, so they make this law so that all the farmers have to pay. And it's very sad. It shouldn't be this way.

Sarah: *I'm wondering if there is poverty in your society.*

Berito: All of us U'wa, equally, are very poor. There's nobody who has more money than anybody else. There's not this inequality. We U'wa believe that if one person has more money or more land or food than someone else, they need to help them. That's part of our culture. The poor help those who are even more poor.

The government wants to have forty thousand million dollars in its bank. The bank that we have is the Earth. We have always said that we don't want to enter the culture of money. Why? Because then there's this mountain of money that only some people have. Tomorrow we will fight over that money, brother against brother. No, that simply doesn't work. We respect many things. We don't kill each other.

Sarah: *What would you like to ask people who hear your story?*

Berito: It would be good if people understood the organizational structures of the indigenous people of the world. The organizations of the indigenous world are the most ancient structures of the world, and they have a kind of intelligence that is very concrete and complete. They don't sell themselves for anything.

Talking with other indigenous organizations from around the world, we know that we are on an equal footing with them because it is our hearts that lead us. The heart is what gives us the intelligence that we shouldn't rule the world. The ceremony encapsulates it all. All the world has ceremonies, and it is these ceremonies that protect Mother Earth.

I think that if the petroleum companies continue to exploit the petroleum they will take all of the strength and spirit out of Mother Earth, and if they do that, we're all going to die. They don't want to make any laws to defend the Earth, like the laws of the indigenous peoples. That's why I said to one of these petroleum men, "Take all of that money you make and stuff it into the Earth and see if it sustains life. That money won't sustain anyone."

Juliet Schor, senior lecturer at Harvard University, is the author of *The Overspent American: Upscaling, Downshifting, and the New Consumer* – which was the inspiration for this roundtable – and before that, *The Overworked American: The Unexpected Decline of Leisure.*

The Overspent American

Juliet Schor and other voluntary simplicity advocates say it's tough to "live simply, so others can simply live." But kicking the overconsumption/overwork addiction is worth the effort.

Sarah van Gelder: *Juliet, what inspired you to write* The Overspent American? *Was it an outgrowth of your previous book on overwork?*

Juliet Schor: When I was traveling around the US after the publication of *The Overworked American*, I was struck by how many people asked me questions about how to escape from the work-and-spend cycle. I wrote this book both to explore the barriers that are keeping people from scaling back on consumption and to look at the factors that might make it easier to downscale.

Sarah: *Most economists would argue that the work-and-spend cycle is exactly what you want in a healthy economy. What concerns you about this dynamic?*

Juliet: First, it requires too many hours of human labor and undermines the quality of life for that reason. Second, it is ecologically unsustainable.

Betsy Taylor is founder and executive director of the Center for a New American Dream, which promotes sustainable lifestyles in the US.

Vicki Robin is co-author of the bestselling book *Your Money or Your Life*, president of the New Road Map Foundation, and an international speaker on financial integrity and sustainability.

Third, it does not yield happiness. Fourth, it is changing our culture in undesirable ways.

Sarah: You talk about the ratcheting up of our standard of "necessity"; what was once considered a luxury becomes something we need. What causes this expectations inflation?

Juliet: The key factors, in my mind, have been the worsening of the income distribution, the growing prominence of television and the resulting decline of sociability, the increasing pressures of jobs (which make people spend compensatorily), the ubiquity of shopping opportunities, and the loss of meaning in Americans' lives.

I think it's also useful to look at the effects of "reference groups," those people (real and fictitious) against whom we measure our own consumption levels. They help form our aspirations and the degree to which we are satisfied with what we have.

Reference groups used to be mainly composed of people near us in the social hierarchy. But people now are more likely to take the top 20 percent of the income distribution as an aspirational target. TV and the media have been important in this by giving us "TV friends" to compare ourselves to, who are almost all affluent.

This has created a strong "aspiration gap" – the gap between what one has and can afford and what one aspires to. Being "middle class" is no longer enough.

Sarah: You talk about denial in your book – denial that the US is a class society and becoming more so all the time. Denial about the role of debt and status in our life. Juliet, could you say more about the nature of this denial and its impacts? Then I'd like to open this to others in the roundtable.

Juliet: I believe Americans continue to overspend in part because it allows us to paper over conflicts, to avoid dealing with ugly status and class issues and many of the dysfunctional aspects of our financial lives. Sixty percent of the families in America can maintain their standards of living for only one month if their income disappears. The next 20 percent can maintain it for only three months. That means that 80 percent of the population is living at an incredibly high level of economic insecurity every day, whether or not they're consciously aware of it.

Betsy Taylor: It's interesting that the biggest blockbuster movie we have at the moment is *Titanic*. On some level, I think it captures the story of our times: High living in the moment. Tremendous faith in technological fixes. Denial of warnings. Repeated avoidance of signs of trouble. A final catastrophe. This seems to be a story that deeply resonates with people in the late 20th century.

Vicki Robin: A recent feature on NBC Nightly News cited the following statistics:
• We have $1.24 trillion in consumer debt – an all time high.
• Personal bankruptcy is up over 400 percent since 1980 (1.3 million people declared bankruptcy in 1997).
• 1.02 million Americans are behind in their mortgage payments.
These are hard numbers that reflect the kind of denial Juliet is citing.

I would add that the advent of "unsecured debt" in the form of credit cards has fed this cycle. If you pay at the minimum rate of 3 percent, a $2,000 purchase at 18.5 percent interest will take 14 years to pay off and cost an extra $1,900.

Duane Elgin is author of *Voluntary Simplicity*, *Awakening Earth* and *Promises Ahead*. He also recently published two reports entitled *Collective Consciousness and Cultural Healing* and *Global Consciousness Change*.

Duane Elgin: Someone once observed that people live by stories, including nations, and that if you can control people's stories, you don't need to control their armies or legislatures, because you already control their minds and hearts.

In the US, television tells most of the people most of the stories about most of the world most of the time. It's not just the thousands of ads for products;

they are more fundamentally watching thousands of ads for a "work-and-spend lifestyle." Never do we see ads for simple living, for future generations, other species, the rain forest, or the ozone layer.

It is not enough to turn off the TV. This medium is far too powerful in shaping our collective consciousness to ignore. The one-dimensional mindset of the mass media is diverting our cultural attention, dumbing-down our potential, and holding back our evolution.

Sarah: *Let's talk more about future generations. Juliet points out that many parents are most concerned about "keeping up with the Jones" in areas affecting their kids. On the other hand, many adults are turned off by kids' materialism. Is there a backlash against consumerism involving kids?*

Betsy: Many people are opting to work and earn less primarily to gain more time with their children. As boomers begin to downshift and cut back, advertisers are turning more intensively to children. A recent report documented efforts to gain brand name identification among children starting at age two.

I am a mother of a seven- and a nine-year-old, and they heavily influence my perspective on life. I think parents are buying things for their kids in part out of a sense of fear about the future. Even my educated and affluent peers seem to feel they have minimal control over anything except their immediate family situations, and they are determined to give their children the maximum advantages possible. This involves the over-programming of children in an endless array of enrichment and sports programs along with the tendency to buy kids the latest technology, toys, and educational tools, all to give your child the competitive edge.

This same fear drives parents to stay in the high-earning careers that guarantee financial security for children, even when these careers often rob children of precious time with their parents.

Juliet: What a crazy system it is in which huge numbers of people are so fearful about failure and do so many crazy things on this account. I already see it in my son's first grade – the intense pressures on children and young teens to do well in school is pretty frightening. One of the key things to ask ourselves is what kind of structure we are creating in which only a few succeed

– and in which those who do "succeed" are likely to be over-worked and miserable?

It's important to fight the trends in the global economy that are creating this kind of insecurity, rather than looking to this privatized solution of cramming kids full of computers and extra-curriculars – basically starting a productivity drive with kids at the age of two!

John de Graaf: There does seem to be a race to provide "enriching" experiences for kids. Some child psychologists, such as David Elkind, author of the *Hurried Child*, suggest we're doing a lot of damage to kids by overcrowding them with structured, adult-supervised activities. Kids' sports, for example, have become so over-organized.

When I was a kid, my buddies and I met at the park, picked teams, made our own ground rules, and played baseball and football and other sports informally. I think it provided good lessons in organizing activities, taking leadership, and getting along with each other. Now, the sports are all controlled by adults.

Wanda Urbanska: I do think kids are receptive to the message of frugality; they're aware that they have too much. John and I certainly saw this when we filmed sixth graders at Jones Elementary School here in Mount Airy, North Carolina, last year for *Escape from Affluenza*.

We were astounded at the level of interest in simple living among the kids. They knew they had too many clothes while their counterparts in the Third World had too few. They could get rid of 80 percent of what was in their closet and not notice the difference. The students were attracted to the "old ways" and recounted with pride how much food their grandparents grew in their summer gardens.

Sarah: *More and more stuff, and less and less security! It's ironic that fear of the future would cause us to overspend,*

Cecile Andrews is the author of T*he Circle of Simplicity: Return to the Good Life* and a speaker on voluntary simplicity.

John de Graaf is co-producer of the PBS specials *Affluenza* and *Escape from Affluenza*.

Wanda Urbanska is co-author of *Simple Living: One Couple's Search for a Better Life* and *Moving to a Small Town: A Guidebook for Moving from Urban to Rural America*.

work hard to project an image of success, and live on the edge financially –
thereby in fact making us less secure.

Cecile Andrews: When I quit my job as a community college administrator, one of my first thoughts was, "I won't have a title! Who will I be?" A few months after quitting, I attended a very expensive wedding, and I had real difficulty knowing how to answer the question, "What do you do?"

Juliet talks in her book of the necessity to maintain an *image* of success (which requires consumerism), because we fear that we could so easily become unemployed. Of course we feel insecure! We just have to look at the homeless to remind us of what could happen to us.

People's concern for projecting an image represents an underlying insecurity – a feeling that we are alone in a universe that doesn't care about us. So consumerism is, in some sense, a substitute for being cared for.

In a way, it's like the early Puritan idea that being "successful" proved that someone was "saved." "Success" meant God must have smiled on them – they were safe and saved. So to reduce consumerism, we need to deal with the insecurity and the pressure to project an image of success.

Juliet: I think that a lot of the symbolic power of consumption is perpetuated through the requirements not to talk about these things. These symbols of success are transmitted nonverbally – the designer logo, the right cosmetics, or the choice of a vacation send certain signals. These are always a little bit under the surface. So I think bringing these associations out into the open, making them visible, and verbalizing the symbols is crucial to giving individuals more freedom to choose not to buy into these symbols.

The anxiety many people feel about their financial future is very paralyzing; it makes people feel out of control. There *are* some things individuals can do. You can reduce or eliminate debt, increase savings, gain marketable skills, and learn to provide for a higher fraction of your total consumption expenditures yourself. You can get your own financial situation and lifestyle into a place where you can weather things like the loss of a job.

Wanda: Many people assume that when Frank and I left our fast-lane life in Los Angeles, we came home to run this orchard with a sizable nest egg – as if people in their right minds could never take such a significant risk without one.

Actually, we didn't have money in the bank – just a strong sense that our lives were out of whack and needed an overhaul. But after 12 years of hard work and simple living, we're on much more solid financial footing than we ever were in with our high-paying jobs.

I've found that being less consumed with earning money gives me more time for building security through "human infrastructure." It takes time to build and maintain friendships, but I believe that people provide the best kind of security.

Let me give an example. I have a friend Marion who had been a high school English teacher in Virginia for many years when she got into a difficult political situation. I could see she was miserable, but she was reluctant to leave. I urged her to apply at the schools here in Mount Airy and made some calls on her behalf. She was offered a job, made the move, and has been much happier for it. She has also acted on my behalf when I needed help.

That kind of caring, hands-on interaction doesn't happen when your daily schedule is overloaded, when there's no time for reflection or action.

Sarah: *What would you say is the biggest, not-to-be missed opportunity for moving to a more sustaining way of life? What one factor have you seen that gives you the most hope that making this shift is possible?*

Duane: I think it is transformative to simply withdraw from the preoccupations with the rat race of accumulation. It is radical simplicity to affirm that our happiness cannot be purchased and that we can accept ourselves as we are. We can affirm that each of us is endowed with a dignity, beauty, and character whose natural expression is infinitely more interesting and engaging than any identity we might construct with stylish clothes and cosmetics.

Betsy: I believe living a life that involves meditation, reflection, and/or prayer is the single greatest factor in moving to more balanced sustainable lifestyles. I think quiet retreat from the dominant culture is vital. I also think that individuals are incapable of staying the course alone, so I think supportive communities and groups are vital.

Cecile: I think the "not-to-be-missed" opportunity is involvement! We must have personal change, yes, but the simplicity movement must go beyond that to working toward something larger. It might be co-housing, eco-villages, "time-dollar"/bartering groups, neighborhood organizations, environmental organizations, churches. Some group that keeps your spirit alive and makes a difference.

My solution, of course, is simplicity circles – a place were people can make real contact with others and gain the courage to express their real selves in the rest of their lives. Then they have a better chance of resisting the forces of our consumer society.

Wanda: A friend of mine from Los Angeles refuses to ever wear anything with brand labeling or identification on the outside, not a logoed T-shirt or a brand-name pair of shoes. And that might be an idea worth bandying about. Try asking a bunch of teenagers to dress for a week without showing a single label. That would be a challenge!

John: Not to be missed opportunities: Talk about the big picture – the connections between our purchases and the workers who produce them, the environment, our own personal stress, our family relations, and the community. Use humor, and realize that this issue speaks to Left and Right alike. I do think we're having an impact, so keep up the great work, everyone!

Vicki: At the New Road Map Foundation, we are shaping our message currently around stress and savings (which are linked).

Money not spent equals resources conserved, both human hours at work and the natural environment.

Savings equals peace of mind and strength, both personal and national (less dependence on foreign investment).

Energy devoted to a full spectrum of meaningful activities – work, family, friends, community, worship – makes for human well-being.

The amazing part of this work on consumption is that, since it is the centerpiece of our culture and economy, it is also a powerful place to work for systemic change. You can press anywhere and move the mountain.

Mark Ludak

Diverse, Green, Beautiful Cities

Carl Anthony is founder and executive director of Urban Habitat Program, convener of the Bay Area Alliance for Sustainable Development, and former president of the Earth Island Institute.

Who wins when sprawl gobbles up open space, freeways slice up neighborhoods, and the inner city is abandoned? Could suburban Whites *and* urban Blacks benefit from a redesign of our cities?

Sarah van Gelder: *Tell me about your background. You are an architect and you were also a civil rights activist. What is the connection?*

Carl Anthony: Originally, my focus was on certain rundown, inner-city neighborhoods. These were places where you'd see miles and miles of commercial strips, but even something as simple as a place to buy decent food was missing. It struck me that although these inner-city neighborhoods were showing obvious signs of neglect, many of them were originally quite beautiful. So I was very much inspired to try to visualize alternatives. I had visions of rebuilding communities to meet the basic needs of the people who live there with parks, daycare centers, and new employment centers that people could walk to.

Sarah: *You've said that sprawl degrades not only farmland and open space but urban life. How did this pattern of sprawl develop? And who wins and loses?*

Carl: A turning point for cities came after World War II, when money became available to build freeways. At the same time, through the Federal Housing Administration and other mortgage institutions, government began financing opportunities for people to buy houses in suburban areas. During much of this time, this housing was really available only to white families because of various discriminatory real estate practices. The result was an incredible metropolitan expansion that filtered Black people and poor people into the inner cities and middle-class and working-class White people out to the suburban fringe. Schools and other public services – swimming pools and parks and libraries – were newer and often of better quality in suburban communities than they were in the inner-city communities that were left behind.

So the kind of polarization developed that was underscored in the Kerner Report in 1968, which found that our society was becoming two separate societies, one Black and one White.

Sarah: *Your report, "What If We Shared," has a sentence I found especially intriguing. It says, "As long as some parts of the region can exclude the costs and effects of social responsibilities, the region's resources will naturally flow there." Can you explain what dynamic is at work there?*

Carl: Well, basically, there are some communities that get the lion's share of public and private investment. Investment in commercial and retail activity tends to go to those neighborhoods where people have more discretionary income. If you wanted to open up an ice cream parlor, for example, you would rather open it in a neighborhood where there is a lot of money. The result is an increasing pattern of concentration of wealth and resources in those places that are already advantaged.

These advantaged areas not only have more taxes to spend – which are invested in schools and other amenities – but they also have lower social needs. So with lower social needs and more taxes, these communities gain more privileges and that reinforces their sense of being different from the rest of society. The issue of race makes this sense of separation even worse.

Sarah: *So there was disinvestment of both private and public money? You always hear about government spending going to inner-city neighborhoods.*

Carl: Take for example the National Highway Defense Act. Until very recently, every time you bought a dollar's worth of gas, four cents would go into a highway trust fund designed to maintain and build freeways. This was a hidden cost we all paid that subsidized sprawl. Likewise, new sewer lines, schools, and other infrastructure that make it possible to build spread-out communities are all major public investments in the development of the city fringe.

There's an assumption that a lot of public monies have gone to support various kinds of empowerment zones and other initiatives in the inner city, but far more public dollars go to support suburban sprawl.

Sarah: *You've talked about cities and land use as issues that bring together the interests of White blue-collar people from the inner suburbs, environmentalists, and inner-city residents. Could you talk about what interests those groups have in common and what the prospects are for them to come together?*

Carl: First of all, current patterns of suburban sprawl and inner city abandonment are totally unsustainable. Land in our metropolitan regions is being squandered at a rate that is much faster than the population growth rate. For example, between 1970 and 1990, the population of metropolitan Los Angeles grew by 48 percent while the land area grew by *300 percent*. In some cities – Cleveland and St. Louis, for example – the population of the metropolitan region actually *declined* while the city was expanding.

This pattern of development requires more roads and clearing farm land. A lot of money is spent building new freeways, office parks, parking lots, and shopping malls on the suburban fringe – in places you can't get to without a car – while the buildings and infrastructure that already exist in the inner city are abandoned. In Philadelphia, for example, there are 20,000 vacant lots and 16,000 vacant buildings located in the center part of the city near to public transportation corridors.

This development pattern not only squanders land, buildings, and infrastructure, but also energy resources; 79 percent of the money spent in the petroleum economy is for transportation.

Sprawl depletes biodiversity, destroys open space on the metropolitan fringe, and lowers air quality because of increased automobile traffic. Increased traffic also pollutes the water; 60 percent of the pollution in the San Francisco

Bay comes from runoff from streets and highways. So environmentalists have an interest in finding ways to rebuild our cities in balance with nature.

Sarah: *I think a lot of people who live outside cities in houses with large yards and lots of trees around may think they are closer to nature and that they are therefore living more sustainable lives.*

Carl: It's a real paradox because, in fact, your ecological footprint *[the land it takes to supply the resources you use and absorb the waste you create—ed.]* is much bigger if you live in one of those comfortable suburban communities; your consumption of water including the lawn, swimming pool, showers is about 500 gallons a day. If you live in north Oakland or in an inner-city neighborhood, you use about 40 gallons a day, and if you're homeless, you use about 5-6 gallons a day. People may feel like they're being more environmentally in tune outside the cities, but actually there's a lot more waste in these communities.

Sarah: *If both environmentalists and inner-city residents have an interest in stopping sprawl, what's preventing them from working together?*

Carl: In the inner cities, the problem is that people have tended to see jobs and economic development as a social, political, and economic issue, and not as an environmental issue. And environmentalists tend to see their issues as being separate from the social and racial justice issues. But actually, they are operating in the same universe; in fact, they are two sides of the same coin.

All that is blocking a coalition between environmentalists and the inner city is the way we think. I sometimes call it an "apartheid of consciousness." We have one set of issues on one side of our head and another set on the other side of our head.

To the extent that we can begin to see that there is a strong relationship between protecting the natural world and bringing the beauty of nature back into cities, and developing healthier racial and social institutions and attitudes, then the two interests can be aligned.

Sarah: *There is another group that you have also included in your coalition-building work isn't there?*

Carl: That's right. The blue-collar, suburban communities have been left out of both the discourse of environmentalists and those advocating social justice. And yet, their communities are suffering both environmentally and economically. In some of these communities, there has been a backlash against affirmative action and other progressive racial policies. However, many of these communities are also suffering from economic decline, and we can see that one of the reasons they are upset is because their voices are not heard.

It is an obvious step to acknowledge their hardship, and instead of competing with working class European-Americans, it makes more sense to realize that everybody can have a better quality of life if we invest in some of these blue-collar suburban communities and maintain their attractiveness and their capacity to meet basic human needs

Sarah: It sounds like a very interesting political opportunity and also a huge challenge to bring those three groups together.

Carl: I guess from where I sit, there's nowhere else to go. We don't have the luxury of pretending we are not all connected. We have no problem in the poorest communities explaining why we think it's necessary to adopt policies that basically are necessary to the survival of life on the planet. There are also a lot of folks who are really concerned about protecting farmland. And we have hungry people in the inner city who are taking over vacant land to create community gardens. Suddenly the language between the people who live in the inner city and the farmers is not the language of polarization – it's a shared language of seeds and soil quality.

Even the business community is finding that our current growth patterns are dysfunctional. An entry-level employee in Silicon Valley making $60,000 per year can't afford to buy a house within two hours of work. Business leaders are realizing that unless they do something about this, they're not going to be able to attract employees.

Sarah: How would you envision the land-use patterns of the Bay Area evolving over time if things were to go as you would like them to?

Carl: I'd like to see a growth boundary around the metropolitan perimeters so that there is a sharp line between the land that is open space and farmland, and land that is built up. I would like to see transit-oriented development, which means that around the public transit stations there is a nucleus of human activity, including employment centers, places for people to live, and retail and commercial activity that is pedestrian friendly.

I would like to see nature brought back into the city, which means uncovering the creeks and waterways that are now covered over. I would like to see reinvestment in parks and open spaces, particularly along areas like the Bay that belong to everybody.

I would like to see higher-density, well-designed housing in strategic locations, but also a great deal more variety and choice in building types. For example, if houses were permitted to have granny-units or in-law units and rent out portions of their house or use parts as an office, you would have a more efficient use of the existing footprint and more options for affordable housing.

I'd like to see brownfields – abandoned toxic places – cleaned up and reused as parks and urban farms and sites for housing and commercial activity. There are 450,000 abandoned brownfield sites of all sizes in the US. I think the challenge is to recycle the urban land and to invest in those neighborhoods and in the people who live there.

Sarah: *The policies that we've been discussing would tend to put more resources into the inner cities and could drive up prices and displace people who have long lived in these neighborhoods. What is your take on how you prevent gentrification?*

Carl: There's a whole history of dealing with this. Jane Jacobs says that there's a difference between gradual money and cataclysmic money. If you have cataclysmic projects that tear down the existing structures and replace them with something new, you tend to destroy the intimate relationship that people have with their surroundings. On the other hand, if the capital invested grows gradually, it tends to strengthen the incumbent communities and organizations.

There's a lot of experience around the country on gentrification. Certain local communities have enacted fees, so if you sell a house within five years of when you bought it, you have to pay a penalty. But the gentrification issue is going to be a big one. It's already being felt in the Mission District. One of the reasons that people want to live in the Mission is that it has a high level of transportation access, wonderful restaurants, bookstores, and cultural institutions, which a typical suburban community doesn't have. But some existing suburban communities *could* have those amenities. Rather than three or four neighborhoods like the Mission in the Bay Area, I'd like to see hundreds of them throughout the region. Some of the older suburban communities could be quite wonderful neighborhoods.

Sarah: *If they were turned into more urban neighborhoods?*

Carl: More urban, but also more wonderful. For example, Pacifica is located on the Pacific Ocean; it's kind of a blue-collar community that's very difficult to get to. It would be a wonderful place to live if there were better transportation access.

We have to try to organize these various communities to face these challenges, because we can't keep losing two acres of farmland a minute in the US while racking up bills for new freeways, schools, sewers, and other infrastructure that we'll still be paying for a hundred years from now.

We can't just continue growing the economy and thinking that benefits will "trickle down" on the poorest communities. As the economy expands, people are getting poorer, and they actually end up taking on the burdens, the externalities, of the growth process. So we can't keep going in that direction.

We've had some luck with collaborative work in the Bay Area. Ten military bases closed with the last round of military base closures, and we've developed reuse plans for most of them through collaboration between many jurisdictions – so far, with no major lawsuits!

The only way to solve our problems is to have an enlightened citizenry that is able to sort through these issues and who are not at each other's throats. In some ways, necessity is the mother of invention. We need more racial and cultural harmony, more respect for nature, and more capacity to address these tough questions.

Paul Hawken is a businessman, founder of The Natural Step–US, author of *The Ecology of Commerce*, and co-author with Amory and Hunter Lovins of *Natural Capitalism*.

Corporate Futures

Some corporate leaders say they want to protect the environment and human rights. Can they be helpful? Or is the corporate structure and its capacity to concentrate power and wealth at the core of the problem?

Sarah van Gelder: *You both seem to agree that a market economy is the best possible system for a number of reasons centering on the creativity, flexibility, resilience of the market, and its capacity to harness human ingenuity. You speak about capitalism in very different ways, however – David describes it as a cancer on the market system, while Paul has been giving the term a new twist by suggesting that capitalism is a good idea, we just haven't really tried it yet. Are these differences in definition, or are there some real underlying disagreements?*

David Korten: I suspect definitions are the key here. So far as I am aware, Paul, the major difference between us is that you have chosen to focus on changing the system of business from within, while I've chosen to focus on working with citizen movements.

Sarah rightly points out, however, that we have substantial differences in how we use the term capitalism. By my understanding, the term came into use in the mid-1800s to refer to an economic and social regime in which the ownership and benefits of capital are appropriated by the few to the exclusion of the many who through their labor make capital productive. This seems to describe all too well the reality of the present global system of business.

I've chosen to take on the role of the small boy in the story "The Emperor's New Clothes" and break the embarrassed silence to affirm that capitalism is about naked greed and is the mortal enemy of markets, democracy, and ethical values. It turns out that this is a very empowering message for most people as it affirms what they have suspected to be true all along.

I am guessing, Paul, that since you are working to win over leaders within the system who have an almost religious attachment to the term capitalism, you find it more effective to embrace the term, while making the case that what we need is a "different kind of capitalism." Working with different constituencies may require the use of different language, even when the ultimate goal is much the same.

Paul Hawken: Capitalism as conventionally defined is a system where the means of production are privately held rather than being in hands of the state. I agree with David that financial capitalism, the capitalism that is in place and practiced, is bizarre and cancerous.

Capitalism arose from industrialism without any particular framework or values. It was sometimes given lofty virtues by observers, much as conservatives do to this day, but social and environmental values were never intrinsic. Capitalism simply emerged. No one said, wouldn't it be cool to have a juggernaut economy of unprecedented productive capacity that destroys the capacity of every living system on Earth, where over 90 percent of the world's wealth would be concentrated in the hands of 2 percent of the people, and the other 98 percent wouldn't mind because they were being anesthetized by shopping or the eventual prospect of having more material goods.

My comment that capitalism might be a good idea is a rhetorical jab at the extreme

David Korten is author of *The Post-Corporate World: Life After Capitalism* and *When Corporations Rule the World.* He is also chair of the board of the Positive Futures Network, publisher of *YES!*

internal contradictions of the present system. It is, in Hazel Henderson's words, a system where the divine rights of kings have been replaced by the divine rights of capital (money).

It is true that I work with corporations, but only in an educational role. I try to inform them, just as I do with my writings. It is always a surprise that a few corporations listen. The number that are truly receptive can be counted on one hand. I am constantly confronted with skepticism and resistance. What little effect I do have is because David and many others are working from the outside. The main reason most companies accept the need for change is because the alternatives are worse. Usually, those alternatives are being fashioned by citizen groups who are addressing corporate hegemony and arrogance through numerous initiatives including boycotts, protests, teach-ins, community activism, shareholder resolutions, Web sites, etc.

But I think David and others working in the area of globalization raise a very important issue. Are corporations as they are constituted reformable? Certainly, there are specific companies, as I mentioned in the *Ecology of Commerce*, that should be grounded and have their licenses taken away. They have such miserable historical records that, were they individuals, they would have been jailed years ago.

But putting aside the true miscreants, can "normal" transnational corporations perform an honorable role? Almost every fiber of my being says no. Yet they are here. That is the dilemma. In this area, I believe David's work is far more important than my own.

I am certain of only one thing: that business as we know it is destroying the Earth, including all cultures and living systems, and never before has there been a system so ubiquitous, so destructive, and so well managed. It is our creation.

However, I don't work to win over corporate leaders. I am a terrible salesman and a worse diplomat. Companies still get angry when I give speeches. I gave a keynote in San Diego recently where the person who introduced me was so apoplectic at the end of my talk he wouldn't speak to me and complained bitterly to the program chairman who had invited me. There are a few CEOs who have changed their corporations rather dramatically and have credited me, which is very kind, but in every case these are people who were already true visionaries and just needed some good information.

Sarah: *Paul, I don't think you're giving yourself enough credit. Influencing a handful of business leaders, indeed! Here is my second question: Where do you see opportunities for change? Gandhi spoke of two parts to a strategy for change – resisting what's not working and creating the new. Do you see evidence of hope in either or both of these areas? Particularly, do you see ways to go beyond making some modifications at the edges to a shift in the entire dynamic?*

David: I have to agree with Sarah that influencing a handful of corporations is an important accomplishment. An effective strategy for change as profound as that we now face must involve many approaches. One among them is to put to a serious test, with an open and honest public accounting, the proposition that the existing system provides corporations the scope to take the lead toward creating a socially and environmentally viable economy.

Ever since I heard about The Natural Step, it struck me that it was a vehicle for providing just such a test because it sets high and uncompromising standards. Paul, you brought the Natural Step to the United States and invited widespread corporate participation. While I'm not surprised to learn that few responded, that information is an important contribution toward a realistic assessment of the often heard claim that corporations will lead the way to social and environmental health if government will just remove the regulatory barriers that hamper responsible behavior. [*See page 63 for more on The Natural Step.*]

With regard to your question, Sarah, until we have a reasonable idea of where we want to go, we are unlikely to get there. I believe we need to move toward a mindful market economy – one that is self-organizing, democratically accountable to all people, rewards productive behavior, provides a decent means of livelihood for every person, encourages ethical behavior, and functions in a balanced and sustainable relationship with the other living systems of our planet. In short, it is an economy that is nearly the mirror opposite of a global economy centrally managed by global corporations larger than most states in response to the demands of financial speculators who make no contribution to productive output.

So far as I can see a mindful market economy has no need for institutions created for the sole purpose of enriching the already wealthy and concentrating economic power without democratic accountability. The problems arise from a combination of size, ownership, and accountability and are best resolved by replacing the global publicly traded, limited liability corporation with human-scale, stakeholder-owner enterprises that are accountable to the communities in which they are located. Nor is there any place in such an economy for financial speculation.

Eliminating financial speculation and the corporation as we know it will not solve all our problems, but it would be a good start. Unfortunately, such an agenda seems rather fanciful given current power realities. On the other hand, given the rate at which our existing economic institutions are destroying life to make money, our very existence depends on turning a seemingly impossible agenda into a feasible and obvious choice.

Paul: The global industrial system is both megalithic and fragile. I suppose I see it in a Dickensian way, with both the best and worst becoming more manifest. The worst we hardly need to talk about. As to the best, worldwide, there are tens of thousands of NGOs that are addressing the issue of sustainability in its broadest and most complete sense. Domestically, my guess is that there are some 30,000 groups. They address a broad array of issues including environmental justice, ecological literacy, public policy, conservation, women's rights and health, population, renewable energy, corporate reform, labor issues, climate change, trade issues, ethical investing, ecological tax reform, water, and much more. These groups conform to both of Gandhi's imperatives: Some resist while the others create new structures, patterns, and means.

The groups tend to be local, marginal, poorly funded and overworked. It is hard for most groups not to feel that they could perish in a twinkling, and a palpable sense of anxiety is there. At the same time, there is a deeper pattern that is extraordinary. Around the world, organizations working on sustainability are creating conventions, declarations, lists of principles, and frameworks that are remarkably in accord. These include the CERES Principles, The Natural Step, Agenda 21, the UN Charter on Human Rights, the Cairo Conference, The Siena Declaration, and thousands more. Never before in history have independent groups from around the world derived frameworks of knowledge that are utterly consonant and in agreement. It is not that they are the same; it is that they do not conflict. This hasn't happened in politics, not in religion, not in psychology, not ever. As external conditions continue to change and worsen socially, environmentally, and politically, organizations working towards sustainability increase, deepen, and multiply. Some day, these dots are going to be connected.

Business reform and restorative economics is only a part of this broader movement towards change. But it is critical.

It is frustrating to see the juggernaut of corporatism continue to concentrate ownership in the media, energy, transportation, publishing, apparel, and so much more and not feel like power is being swept away and sequestered into the hands of the few. Although the rate of corporate change is accelerating now, sometimes you have to bite your lip when you see what passes for change. Is an institution making a legitimate effort to transform its culture and direction or is it just standing on the first wrung of the ladder for a better view? Sometimes, even they don't know; it is all so new and bewildering. When you get an organization like Monsanto completely prostituting the concept of sustainability, that understandably raises the level of cynicism as other corporations announce that they are moving in that direction.

We are talking about some very entrenched and highly reinforced paradigms that have been drilled into the head of every MBA in America, not to mention overseas. They're not easy to change. Even CEOs who do understand sustainability extraordinarily well, like Ray Anderson, say that they have a difficult time being understood by other CEOs. Those barriers permeate the organization, not just top management. Nevertheless, it is the executive suite that poses the greatest barrier. Short attention spans, gnawing stress, compensation incentives (which are all essentially short term), ecological and biological illiteracy, investor demands, peer pressure, glass ceilings and gender bias (we are talking about a profoundly male view of the world), political conservatism – all create a formidable wall of resistance.

I agree with David's view that we are goal-less. What are the goals of corporate America? Strip away the platitudes and what do you have left?

One of the most humorous aspects of teaching The Natural Step in corporations is when you come to the Fourth System Condition, the part that says that without social justice and fair and equitable distribution of resources there can be no such thing as sustainability. Business people go ballistic. They think it is socialist, communist, the nose of the leftist camel slipping under the tent. Literally, some are repulsed by it. We are in a country that was founded on "liberty and justice for all," and if you raise that issue in the business community, some executives will fall off their chairs. Sometimes, I have asked business people who reject the notion of social justice whether they believe in injustice, inequality, lack of opportunity for women, and unfairness. They protest just as vehemently. So then I ask them what do they believe? What do we believe? What are our goals? It seems to me that our goals have been money – period. We got it. Not very well distributed, but goodness there is a lot of money moving around. So the good news is that when Americans set a goal, they usually achieve it. The problem is that we have such insignificant and petty goals.

I am going on too long here, but maybe a story will suffice. In one of these monolithic and highly resistant corporations which shall remain nameless (but let's just say that I doubt if the readers of *YES!* use one single product from this $9 billion behemoth), a friend was giving a one-day workshop to middle management on sustainability. Now this group had already rejected the Fourth System Condition about social justice and resource equity. They were given an exercise that we do in some of our workshops. Their task was to break into five groups, with each group designing a spaceship (size and propulsion were not issues, and it could receive sunlight from the outside) that would leave the Earth and bring its inhabitants back, alive, happy, and healthy 100 years later. Being engineers, they loved the challenge. At the end, they would vote on which spaceship they would want to travel on, and that would be the winning group.

The winning spaceship was brilliantly designed. Now bear in mind, this company, amongst many other things, makes pesticides and herbicides. Things that kill life, i.e. biocides. On the winning spaceship, they decided that they needed insects so they decided that they would take no pesticides. They knew that photosynthesis was key to their survival. They also decided that weeds were important in a healthy ecosystem and banned herbicides on board. Their food system, in other words, was totally organic. This group of engineers and MBAs also decided that as a crew, they needed lots of singers, dancers, artists, and storytellers, because the CDs and videos would get old and boring fast, and engineers alone did not a village make. There were many more aspects, but two were most interesting. One, they decided that virtually none of the products they were making on Earth would be useful on this spaceship. And, at the end, they were asked if it was okay if 20 percent of the people on the spaceship controlled 80 percent of the resources on board. They immediately and vociferously rejected that notion as unworkable, unjust, and unfair. And then they realized what they had said. In other words, in small groups with appropriate goals and challenges, we know the right things to do. As a society within the world of capitalism, we are not very bright.

Sarah: *Since Paul worked closely with Monsanto for some time and David has met and corresponded with CEO Robert Shapiro, I wonder if you could both reflect on your experiences with Monsanto. What was accomplished and what was behind the company's interest in sustainability?*

Paul: OK, here goes:

Like many others in the environmental movement, I was invited to St. Louis to present issues about sustainability. Although I refused initially, I accepted reluctantly for a simple reason: if Monsanto could change, then any company could.

As far as I can see, there has been little or no change. Whatever plans and products they had in their pipelines came right on through. I don't know of any new products that came about because of any environmental commitment, and the old underlying divisional culture of ramming products into the marketplace without consulting a broader stakeholder community about effects, values, science, and other potential concerns – with the arrogance that entails – remains intact. What exists now is a company without any clear leadership, with divisional heads consistently putting their foot in their mouth, and a product line that is truly unnerving.

I continue to follow their devolution, especially in Europe, where they have become the most reviled American corporation. No small achievement.

It is hard to say, looking back, what their interest in sustainability was. I am assuming that they believed that genetically modified organisms were more sustainable, and that they were looking for some sort of intellectual bulwark to support their life sciences approach. They never found it, of course, and have largely dropped their sustainable development division and any pretense that sustainable is a word or concept that informs their activity.

David: Paul, I strongly share your perception regarding the importance of the convergence of values and visions among citizen groups the world over. We are witness to the emergence of a new form of global leadership from below, grounded in a love of life and a capacity for deep compassion. It points to a powerful, soulful awakening that is our primary source of hope for the future.

By contrast, I've come to realize that those who look to the soulless legal instrument of the corporation as a source of leadership toward restoring the life of planet and community look in the wrong place. The corporation is a creature of money, not life, and as such it will always put money's interests ahead of life's interests.

I was fascinated by your story about the spaceship design exercise. To me it underscores a profound finding from the new biology that just as living beings have a natural drive toward self-preservation, they also have a natural drive to identify with the interests of the larger living communities on which their own function depends.

When corporate executives identify with the interests of the artificial legal entity of the corporation that employs them, they almost inevitably embrace the values and worldview embedded in its legal structure. In this context, concerns for equity and social justice appear alien, naive, and even subversive.

Yet when these same executives engaged in the design exercise, their point of reference shifted from the corporation to the spaceship and its inhabitants. At least temporarily, their values and worldview shifted accordingly – even without their noticing it. Instead of focusing on what will make money, they focused on what is necessary to sustain a healthy living community – a wholly different perspective.

Which brings me to your question, Sarah, about Monsanto, the current poster child of corporate irresponsibility. While I had far less contact with them than Paul, I did have meetings in 1996 with a number of Monsanto's top managers and in 1997 had a private breakfast with Shapiro. They impressed me as wonderful people who seemed deeply committed to using the resources of Monsanto to create a better world for all.

But what can you do when you are running a multi-billion dollar corporation that makes not a single product that any sane individual would want along on a spaceship journey – a corporation that is accountable to a fickle stock market that has doubled the price of your stock during the previous year in the expectation that your sales of genetically engineered products are going to generate rapidly growing profits?

You most likely do what Monsanto's critics accuse it of doing.

If Monsanto were the only corporation prone to advance its interests with a reckless disregard of the human and natural interest, we could simply close it down and be done with the problem. Unfortunately, the Monsanto case is of interest largely because it reveals with such startling clarity how corporate life leads good people to do terrible things. It is a reminder that so long as we work in the employ of a publicly traded corporation, we are paid to generate ever-growing stock prices for corporate shareholders without regard to any other interest – including such fundamental interests as the genetic integrity of planetary life and the survival of the species.

Sarah: *Where do you feel the least certain about your own work and about prospects for the future? What keeps you up at night? And what have you observed that gives you hope? Where do you plan to put your own efforts toward a more just, sustainable, and compassionate world?*

David: I see a growing popular sense that corporations and financial markets are running out of control in highly destructive ways. This is especially true in Europe and many parts of Asia, where people are far more aware of the global financial crisis because they are closer to the consequences. Because the US so dominates the global financial system, we have so far been able live in splendid isolation, passing the burdens of our failed economic policies onto others and then blaming them for the failures these policies have caused.

I believe the key to change is to help people see that there are real alternatives to global capitalism and that these alternatives have nothing whatever in common with Soviet-style communism or other forms of state domination. The idea that our only choices are between rule by unaccountable corporations or unaccountable states is nonsense.

Real markets aren't vicious gladiatorial arenas in which only the biggest and most ruthless survive. They are places where people engage in productive exchange with a mindfulness of their own needs and the needs of the larger community in which they live – the mindful markets I mentioned earlier. Mindful enterprises are owned by real people who function simultaneously as entrepreneurs, workers, and community members. They operate small farms and bakeries, local convenience stores, health food stores, the local hardware or appliance store, and community-oriented bookstores and coffee shops.

They love their communities and their work and are proud to provide good service at reasonable prices.

My own favorite example in the neighborhood where I live is the Bainbridge Island Winery, owned and operated by the warmest, most generous people imaginable. They tend the Earth and the grapes with loving care, produce fine wines, and sell them only from their winery shop so that they come to know their customers, who in turn make a connection between the wine they drink and the land and the people who produce it.

I believe we are seeing the emergence of a new consumer consciousness, a preference for wholesome, locally grown organic foods, and for the producers and merchants who are rooted in their communities and care about a healthy social and natural environment – human-scale, stakeholder-owned, and accountable. My own energies are increasingly directed to helping people recognize and nurture such alternatives and to identifying the critical leverage points by which we can transfer energies from the institutions of global capitalism to the institutions of mindful markets.

Paul: I guess what gives me great foreboding is the prospect that we may in fact be in the middle of what Peter Schwartz calls "The Long Boom," in which economic growth will continue to rocket for years to come, fortunes be piled upon fortunes, where 35-year-old entrepreneurs have a personal net worth of $5 billion because they figured out a way to auction off used Pez dispensers and howitzers on the net, and sage pundits call this the "new economy." Already, a nouveau monetary class is crowding the airwaves and newsstands with the kind of apolitical libertarianism you see in *Wired*, a world in which it will be very hard to discern values of any kind. It is a world where we can become just too clever and hip and cool and find ourselves at the edge of nowhere, dressed to kill, talking on our cell phones, irritatedly waiting for something even newer than what was new yesterday because novelty is the only thing left by which we define ourselves. It doesn't bother me that these things exist, but what keeps me up at night is how growth, money, polarization of income, concentration of power, corporatization of media, and other forces in play will vanquish the breathing space human beings need for discourse, debate, reflection, and democracy.

What is most hopeful in the world today is what is least visible. With the exception of Ray Anderson and a handful of others, I don't see a lot in the corporate arena that is hopeful. I say that just as many companies are becoming more transparent, agreeing to redesign products, embracing 'sustainability,' and more. But there is a powerful dilution of the vision of sustainability that is occurring, and as yet, the incapacity to accept responsibility – in some cases, even culpability – for what we have before us.

What I find hopeful is the work of activists; small, local and bioregional NGOs; environmental educators; the men and women who steward our parks and wild refuges; the newly awakened citizens who finally realize that they are downwind and downriver. I find hope in the steadfastness of spirit that can be seen in the indigenous communities. I see vibrancy in a broad array of citizen movements here and around the world. I see hope in what many think is a pessimistic assessment, that change will not and cannot occur from the center, from Washington, from Wall Street.

I believe we are undergoing a far greater evolution than what is being paid lip service to. I believe we are only seeing the very rudiments and beginnings of that change. I do not expect many of our institutions will exist 100 years from now. I don't say that apocalyptically, only in that I believe they will be abandoned and replaced as people vote with their hearts and feet. The university, the church, and the government have all failed to provide the knowledge, inspiration, and leadership people need to move coherently as a society to a social good.

I have done three things to try to address the damage businesses do. I wrote and talked extensively about the *Ecology of Commerce*, I brought to this country The Natural Step and helped establish it, and have co-authored *Natural Capitalism* with Amory and Hunter Lovins of the Rocky Mountain Institute. For me, that may be enough. I want to work with people who do not use money to measure anything, especially their life. I want to work where there is more heart and less greed, more laughter and less pride, more options and no stock options.

Beyond Greed & Scarcity

Bernard Lietaer helped design the single European currency while at the Central Bank in Belgium. He was also a currency speculator and has consulted on currency issues around the world. His most recent book is *The Future of Money: Beyond Greed and Scarcity.*

Economics doesn't have to be "the dismal science." Bernard Lietaer says we could redesign money to encourage abundance and generosity instead of greed and scarcity.

Sarah van Gelder: *Why are you so interested in alternative currencies?*

Bernard Lietaer: Money is like an iron ring we've put through our noses. We've forgotten that we designed it, and it's now leading us around. I think it's time to figure out where *we* want to go – in my opinion toward sustainability and community – and then design a money system that gets us there.

Sarah: *So you would say that the design of money is actually at the root of much else that happens, or doesn't happen, in society?*

Bernard: That's right. While economic texts say that people and corporations compete for markets and resources, I claim they are competing for money, using markets and resources to do so. So designing new money systems really amounts to redesigning the target that orients much human effort.

Furthermore, I believe that greed and competition are not a result of immutable human temperament. I have come to the conclusion that greed and fear of scarcity are in fact being continuously created and amplified as a direct result of the kind of money we are using. For example, we can produce more than enough food to feed everybody, and there is definitely enough work for everybody in the world, but there is clearly not enough money to pay for it all. The scarcity is in our national currencies. In fact, the job of central banks is to create and maintain that currency scarcity. The direct consequence is that we have to fight with each other in order to survive.

Money is created when banks lend it into existence. When a bank provides you with a $100,000 mortgage, it creates only the principal, which you spend and which then circulates in the economy. The bank expects you to pay back $200,000 over the next 20 years, but it doesn't create the second $100,000 – the interest. Instead, the bank sends you out into the tough world to battle against everybody else to bring back the second $100,000. So when the bank verifies your "creditworthiness," it is really checking whether you are capable of competing and winning against other players – able to extract the second $100,000 that was never created.

All the banks are doing the same thing when they lend money into existence. That is why the decisions made by central banks, like the Federal Reserve in the US, are so important – increased interest costs automatically determine a larger proportion of necessary bankruptcies.

Sarah: *That also influences the unemployment rate.*

Bernard: It's certainly a major factor, but there's more to it. Information technologies increasingly allow us to attain good economic growth without increases in employment. A study by The International Metalworkers Federation in Geneva predicts that within 30 years, 2 or 3 percent of the world's population will be able to produce everything we need on the planet. Even if they're off by a factor of 10, we'd still have a question of what 80 percent of humanity will do.

I believe we're seeing one of the last job-driven affluent periods in the US now. My forecast is that local currencies will become a major tool for social design if for no other reasons than employment. I don't claim that these local currencies will or should replace national currencies; that is why I call them "complementary" currencies. The national competition-generating currencies will still have a role in the competitive global market. I believe, however, that complementary currencies are better suited to developing cooperative, local economies.

Sarah: *And these local economies will provide a form of employment that won't be threatened with extinction?*

Bernard: As a first step, that is correct. For example, in France, there are 300 local exchange networks, called *Grain de Sel*, literally "Grain of Salt." These systems – which arose when the unemployment levels reached about 12 percent – facilitate exchanges of everything from rent to organic produce, but they do something else as well. Every fortnight in the Ariège, in southwestern France, there is a big party. People come to trade not only cheeses, fruits, and cakes as in the normal market days, but also hours of plumbing, haircuts, sailing or English lessons. Only local currencies accepted!

Local currency creates work, and I make a distinction between *work* and *jobs*. A job is what you do for a living; work is what you do because you like to do it. I expect jobs to increasingly become obsolete, but there is still an almost infinite amount of fascinating *work* to be done.

For example, in France you find people offering guitar lessons and requesting lessons in German. Neither would pay in French *francs*. But when people create their own money, they don't need to build in a scarcity factor. And they don't need to get currency from elsewhere in order to have a means of making an exchange with a neighbor.

Edgar Cahn's Time Dollars are a classical example. As soon as you have an agreement between two people about a transaction using Time Dollars, they literally create the necessary "money" in the process; there's no scarcity of money. That does not mean there's an infinite amount of this currency, either; you cannot give me 500,000 hours – nobody has 500,000 hours to give. So there's a ceiling on it, yes, but there's no artificial scarcity. Instead of pitting people against each other, the system actually helps them cooperate.

Sarah: *You're suggesting that scarcity needn't be a guiding principle of our economic system. But isn't scarcity absolutely fundamental to economics, especially in a world of limited resources?*

Bernard: My analysis of this question is based on the work of Carl Gustav Jung because he is the only one with a theoretical framework for collective psychology, and money is fundamentally a phenomenon of collective psychology. A key concept Jung uses is the *archetype*, which can be described as an emotional field that mobilizes people, individually or collectively, in a particular direction. Jung showed that whenever a particular archetype is repressed, two types of shadows emerge, which are polarities of each other.

For example, if my higher self – corresponding to the archetype of the King or the Queen – is repressed, I will behave either as a Tyrant or as a Weakling. These two shadows are connected to each other by fear. A Tyrant is tyrannical because he's afraid of appearing weak; a Weakling is afraid of being tyrannical. Only someone with no fear of either one of these shadows can embody the archetype of the King.

Now let's apply this framework to a well-documented phenomenon – the repression of the Great Mother archetype. The Great Mother archetype was very important in the Western world from the dawn of prehistory throughout the pre-Indo-European time periods, as it still is in many traditional cultures today. But this archetype has been violently repressed in the West for at least 5,000 years starting with the Indo-European invasions – reinforced by the anti-Goddess view of Judeo-Christianity, culminating with three centuries of witch hunts – all the way to the Victorian era. If there is a repression of an archetype on this scale and for this length of time, the shadows manifest in a powerful way in society. After 5,000 years, people will consider the corresponding shadow behaviors as "normal."

The question I have been asking is very simple: What are the shadows of the Great Mother archetype?

I'm proposing that these shadows are greed and fear of scarcity. So it should come as no surprise that in Victorian times – at the apex of the repression of the Great Mother – a Scottish schoolmaster named Adam Smith noticed a lot of greed and scarcity around him and assumed that was how all "civilized" societies worked. Smith, as you know, created modern economics, which can be defined as a way of allocating scarce resources through the mechanism of individual, personal greed.

Sarah: Wow! So if greed and scarcity are the shadows, what does the Great Mother archetype herself represent in terms of economics?

Bernard: Let's first distinguish between the Goddess, who represented all aspects of the divine, and the Great Mother, who specifically symbolizes planet Earth – fertility, nature, the flow of abundance in all aspects of life. Someone who has assimilated the Great Mother archetype trusts in the abundance of the universe. It's when you lack trust that you want a big bank account. The first guy who accumulated a lot of stuff as protection against future uncertainty automatically had to start defending his pile against everybody else's envy and needs. If a society is afraid of scarcity, it will actually create an environment in which it manifests well-grounded reasons to live in fear of scarcity. It is a self-fulfilling prophecy.

We have been living for a long time under the belief that we need to create scarcity to create value. Although that is valid in some material domains, we extrapolate it to other domains where it may not be valid. For example, there's nothing to prevent us from freely distributing information; the marginal cost of information today is practically nil. Nevertheless, we invent copyrights and patents in an attempt to keep it scarce.

Sarah: So fear of scarcity creates greed and hoarding, which in turn creates the scarcity that was feared. Whereas cultures that embody the Great Mother are based on abundance and generosity. Those ideas are implicit in the way you've defined community, are they not?

Bernard: Actually it's not my definition, it's etymological. The origin of the word "community" comes from the Latin *munus*, which means the gift, and *cum*, which means together, among each other. So community literally means to give among each other. Therefore I define my community as a group of people who welcome and honor my gifts, and from whom I can reasonably expect to receive gifts in return.

Sarah: And local currencies can facilitate that exchange of gifts.

Bernard: The majority of the local currencies I know about have been started for the purpose of creating employment, but there is a growing group of people who are starting local currencies specifically to create community.

For example, I would feel funny calling my neighbor in the valley and saying, "I notice you have a lot of pears on your tree. Can I have them?" I would feel I needed to offer something in return. But if I'm going to offer scarce dollars, I might just as well go to the supermarket, so we end up not using the pears. If I have local currency, there's no scarcity in the medium of exchange, so buying the pears becomes an excuse to interact. In Takoma Park, Maryland, Olaf Egeberg started a local currency to facilitate these kinds of exchanges, and participants agree that is exactly what has been happening.

Sarah: Can local currencies also be a means for people to meet their basic needs for food and housing?

Bernard: There are lots of people who love gardening but can't make a living from it in the competitive world. If a gardener is unemployed, and I'm unemployed, in the normal economy we might both starve. However, with complementary currencies he can grow my salads, which I pay for in local currency earned by providing another service to someone else.

In Ithaca, "Hours" are accepted at the farmer's market; the farmers can use the local currency to hire someone to help with the harvest or to do some repairs. Some landlords accept Hours for rent, particularly if they don't have a mortgage that must be paid in scarce dollars.

When you have local currency, it quickly becomes clear what's local and what's not. K-Mart will accept dollars only; their suppliers are in Hong Kong or Singapore or Kansas City. But Ithaca's local supermarket accepts Hours as well as dollars. By using local currencies, you create a bias toward local sustainability.

Sarah: Local currencies also provide communities with some buffering from the ups and downs of the global economy. You've been in the business of monitoring, dealing in, and even helping to design the global finance system. Why would communities want to be insulated from it?

Bernard: First of all, today's official monetary system has almost nothing to do with the real economy. Just to give you an idea, year 2000 statistics indicate that the volume of currency exchanged on the global level is $2 trillion per day. This is many times more than the daily gross domestic product (GDP) of all of the developed countries (OECD) together.

Of that volume, only 2 or 3 percent has to do with real trade or investment; the remainder takes place in the speculative global cyber-casino. This means that the real economy has become relegated to a mere frosting on the speculative cake, an exact reversal of how it was just two decades ago.

As a result, power has shifted irrevocably away from governments toward the financial markets. When a government does something not to the liking of the market – like the British in '91, the French in '94, or the Mexicans in '95 – nobody sits down at the table and says "you shouldn't do this." A monetary crisis simply manifests in that currency. So a few hundred people, who are not elected by anybody and have no collective responsibility whatsoever, decide what your pension fund is worth – among other things.

Sarah: *You mentioned earlier that local currencies help promote local sustainability. What's the connection?*

Bernard: To understand that, we need to see the relationship between interest rates and the ways we discount the future. If I ask, "Do you want $100 now or $100 a year from now," most people would want the money now because one can deposit the money risk-free in a bank account and get about $110 a year later. Another way of putting it is that if I were to offer you $100 a year from now that would be about equal to offering you $90 today. This discounting of the means that under our current system it makes sense to cut down trees and put the money in the bank where it will grow faster than trees. It makes sense to "save" money by building poorly insulated houses because the discounted cost of the extra energy used over the lifetime of the house is cheaper than insulating.

We can, however, design a monetary system that does the opposite; it actually creates long-term thinking through what is called a "demurrage charge." The demurrage charge is a concept developed by Silvio Gesell about a century ago. His idea was that money is a public good – like the telephone or bus transport – and that we should charge a small fee for using it. In other words, we create a negative rather than a positive interest rate. So if I gave you a $100 bill and told you that a month from now you're going to have to pay $1 to keep the money valid, what would you do?

Sarah: *I suppose I would try to invest it in something else.*

Bernard: You got it. You know the expression, "Money is like manure; it's only good when it's spread out." In the Gesell system, people would only use money as a medium of exchange, but not as a store for value. That would create work, because it would encourage circulation, and it would invert the short-term incentive system. Instead of cutting trees down to put the money in the bank, you would want to invest your money in living trees or installing insulation in your house.

Sarah: *Has this ever been tried?*

Bernard: There are only three periods I have found: classical Egypt, about three centuries in the European Middle Ages, and a few years in the 1930s.

In ancient Egypt, when you stored grain, you would receive a token, which was exchangeable and became a type of currency. If you returned a year later with 10 tokens, you would only get nine tokens worth of grain, because rats and spoilage would have reduced the quantities, and because the guards at the storage facility had to be paid. So that amounted to a demurrage charge.

Egypt was the breadbasket for the ancient world, the gift of the Nile. Why? Because instead of keeping value in money, everybody invested in productive assets that would last forever – things like land improvements and irrigation systems. Proof that the monetary system had something to do with this wealth is that it all ended abruptly as soon as the Romans replaced the Egyptian 'grain standard' currency with their own money system, with positive interest rates. After that, Egypt ceased being the grain-basket, and became a "developing country" as it is called today.

In Europe during the Middle Ages – the 10th to 13th centuries – local currencies were issued by local lords, and then periodically recalled and reissued with a tax collected in the process. Again, this was a form of demurrage that made money undesirable as a store of value. The result was the blossoming of culture and widespread well-being, corresponding exactly to the time period when these local currencies were used. Practically all the cathedrals were built during this time period.

If you think about what is required as investment for a small town to build a cathedral, it's extraordinary.

Sarah: *Because cathedrals take generations to build?*

Bernard: Well, not only that. Besides the obvious symbolic and religious roles – which I don't want to belittle – one should remember that cathedrals had an important economic function: they attracted pilgrims, who, from a business perspective, played a similar role to tourists today. These cathedrals were built to last forever and create a long-term cash flow for the community. This was a way of creating abundance for you and your descendants for 13 generations. The proof is that it still works today. In Chartres, for instance, the bulk of the city's businesses still live from the tourists who visit the cathedral 800 years after it was finished!

When the introduction of gunpowder technology enabled the kings to centralize power in the early 14th century, the first thing they did was to monopolize the money system. What happened? No more cathedrals were built. The population was just as devoutly Christian in the 14th or 15th century, but the economic incentive for collective long-term investments was gone.

I use the cathedral simply as an example. Accounts from 12th century estates show that mills and other productive assets were maintained at an extraordinary level of quality, with parts replaced even before they wore out. Recent studies have revealed that the quality of life for the common laborer in Europe was the highest in the 12th to 13th centuries; perhaps even higher than today. When you can't keep savings in the form of money, you invest them in something that will produce value in the future. So this form of money created an extraordinary boom.

Sarah: Yet this was a period when Christianity was supreme in Europe and so presumably the Great Mother archetype was still being repressed.

Bernard: Actually, a very interesting religious symbol became prevalent during this time: the famous "Black Madonna." There were hundreds of these statues during the 10th to 13th centuries, some of which were actually statues of Isis with the child Horus sitting on her lap, directly imported from Egypt during the first Crusades. Her special vertical chair was called the "cathedra" (which is where the word cathedral comes from), and interestingly this chair was the exact symbol identifying Isis in ancient Egypt. The statues of the Black Madonnas were also identified in medieval time as the "Alma Mater" (literally the "Generous Mother," an expression still used in America to refer to someone's 'mother university').

The Black Madonnas were a direct continuity of the Great Mother in one of her most ancient forms. She symbolized birth and fertility, the wealth of the land. She symbolized spirit incarnate in matter, before the patriarchal societies separated spirit from matter. So here we have a direct archetypal linkage between the two civilizations that spontaneously created money systems with demurrage charges while creating unusual levels of abundance for the common people: ancient Egypt and 10th-to-13th century Europe. These money systems correspond exactly to the honoring of that archetype.

Sarah: *What potential do you see for local currencies to bring this Great Mother archetype of abundance and generosity into our economic system today? And what difference would it make if we were successful?*

Bernard: The biggest issues that I believe humanity faces today are sustainability and the inequalities and breakdown in community, which create tensions that result in violence and wars. We can address both these issues with the same tool, by consciously creating currency systems that enhance community and sustainability.

Significantly, we have witnessed in the past decades a re-awakening of the feminine archetype. It is reflected not only in the women's movement, in the dramatic increase in ecological concerns, or in new epistemologies reintegrating spirit and matter, but also in the technologies that enable us to replace hierarchies with networks (such as the Internet).

Add to these trends the fact that for the first time in human history we have available the production technologies to create unprecedented abundance. All this converges into an extraordinary opportunity to combine the *hardware* of our technologies of abundance and the *software* of archetypal shifts. Such a combination has never been available at this scale or at this speed: it enables us to consciously design money to work for us, instead of us *for it*.

I propose that we choose to develop money systems that will enable us to attain sustainability and community healing on a local and global scale. These objectives are in our grasp within less than one generation's time. Whether we actualize them or not will depend on our capacity to cooperate with each other to consciously reinvent our money.

Healing Stories

Rachel Naomi Remen, MD, is medical director of the Commonweal Cancer Help Program and a professor of medicine. This interview took place following the release of her best-selling book *Kitchen Table Wisdom: Stories that Heal.* Her more recent book is *My Grandfather's Blessing.*

A doctor who has lived for years with a chronic and life-threatening disease learns about listening, loving, and opening to the unknown as a path to healing.

Sarah van Gelder: *Let me start by asking about the title that you chose for your book. What does the kitchen table have to do with wisdom?*

Rachel Naomi Remen: *Kitchen Table Wisdom* is about the fact that we are all healers of each other. We have a very wounded world. And it's a world full of experts. Long before there were experts, long before there were psychiatrists and psychologists, we were there for each other. We need to be there for each other again in that same way. I don't think that many of us realize the power of our attention, our caring, and our love.

Sarah: *So you think all those experts are getting in the way of our ability to heal ourselves and each other?*

Rachel: Oh, yes. We've become a highly technological society, and we've given away a lot of our power. I think most people don't recognize that listening is one of the most powerful tools of healing. And they don't realize that when they listen to another person without judgment, the other person may be able to recognize their personal truth for the first time – to know it, to speak it, and also to inhabit it in their lives.

Sarah: *When I first saw the title of your book, I had an image of women passing wisdom along to other women around a kitchen table. And then I read your story about your grandfather.*

Rachel: Most of my early wisdom education took place in the kitchen, under a veil of secrecy, which, of course, made it all the more intriguing for a little girl. My parents were socialists. Religion was viewed as "the opiate of the masses," and science was the answer to all the chaos of life. My grandfather was an orthodox rabbi. He imparted a very traditional and very beautiful wisdom, without telling me its source so that I wouldn't tell my parents.

One of the most powerful things he did was to tell me the stories of Genesis from the perspective of the women in the stories. He told me the story in which Abraham takes Isaac up the mountain because God has asked him to sacrifice his only son, but he told it from Sarah's point of view. He also told me Eve's story, and Rachel's. It was only many, many years later that I heard the official versions. What he was doing was setting up a group of heroic women to inspire me. Women were not second-class citizens; women were people of spiritual substance.

Sarah: *You say in your book that, as a child, you thought becoming an adult and becoming a doctor were essentially the same thing.*

Rachel: My grandfather's sons were all physicians and both daughters were nurses. In two generations of that family there are nine physicians and three nurses. They had a tremendous influence on me. I grew up between those worlds: the world of wisdom and of seeking, and the world of knowledge and of science. I think I've occupied the bridge between those two worlds all of my life.

Sarah: *When you went into medical training, you identified more with the science side. Did you lose track of your grandfather's lessons during that period?*

Rachel: In medical training, you can lose track of your own name! Medical training is one of the most difficult things that anyone ever undergoes. People don't appreciate how extreme it is and how firmly it holds its belief systems; you are exposed to them 20 hours a day, year after year. You come to value factual knowledge, but a good life is based on wisdom, and wisdom is what happens in between the facts.

I remember walking into Bloomingdale's once – on a very rare foray from the hospital – and thinking, "Oh, look at all the patients!" Medical school changes the way you see things, and for some, that perspective never changes back.

Sarah: *It did for you, though. What do you think opened your perspective?*

Rachel: I was fortunate enough in this sense to have a chronic illness. While my teachers were providing me with theories about disease, my illness gave me an understanding of suffering, of disease as experience, not as intellectual construct.

The other thing was that I was one of the few women in my training program, and every time anyone had an emotional response to their disease, I would be called upon. Either the men would ask me about it, or they would actually ask me to come and comfort a patient who was crying. So I got to listen to a lot of patients. First, I was very surprised to find that people with the same disease had such different stories. And the stories I heard! The life in them! No two people have a disease the same way. No two people heal in the same way. And the love in the stories, the suffering, the loss, the courage, the wisdom, and the meaning people found in their suffering was so much more compelling to me than the pathophysiology of the disease.

In those days, no one talked about this kind of thing. Even the psychiatrists were basically interested in mental disease, mental pathology. This was not mental illness; this was human experience with all its power. The only people you could talk to about this were the patients themselves. This is the conversation of people in bomb shelters, where you go far below the surfaces. We would talk about what's important and who we are. And in the end, the patients reminded me of who I was. They healed me.

Sarah: *You talk about "coming to class openhearted," about what you can learn if you stay open, and you also talk about how that can be very painful.*

Rachel: Not as painful as hardening your heart. My friend Dean Ornish refers to cardiac bypass as a metaphor for the way we all live; we have bypassed the heart in this culture, especially middle-aged men. I don't think it's as painful to experience yourself as human as it is to numb yourself and harden yourself. In the end, losing your heart is where real suffering lies, I think.

When you become alienated from yourself and from the world around you, and when you lose your sense of awe – whether at the life of the planet or life in human beings – *that* is suffering. We are still a frontier society, and we carry the values of the frontier – independence, competence, self-sufficiency. The shadow side of that is that we have become so accustomed to loneliness that we don't even know we are lonely. That is real suffering.

Distance and objectivity don't help you avoid wounding and loss; they do prevent you from accessing the human strength to heal losses. Nobody can pray from an objective position. Nobody can weep, nobody can receive comfort from an objective position. We still are wounded, but our objectivity distances us from healing.

Sarah: This openness to compassion affects us on an interpersonal level, but it also affects our understanding of whole classes of people who are in completely different situations from ourselves.

Rachel: You can never feel compassion from knowing the facts; you feel compassion when you know the stories. If we could have heard all of the stories of the Gulf War, our hearts would have broken open. As it was, people were watching smart missiles on television as if it was some kind of a computer game. Without the human stories, there's nothing for us to connect to. We don't connect with the heart and so we do not understand.

Sarah: From what you've learned about healing ourselves individually what do you think can help heal us as a society?

Rachel: I believe that if you want to understand both the strengths and the shortcomings of a culture – its power, its grace, its limitations, its illusions – the place to look is at its medical system, because the medical system concentrates the state of being of the culture around it and reflects it back. The objectivity that we criticize our doctors for, the faith in science as the solution to all of the world's ills – we share those attitudes as a culture.

Often, the shadow of a culture will be reflected in its medical institutions, and when we are confronted with shadow material, we often become very judgmental and critical of whoever presents it to us – a sort of kill-the-messenger phenomenon. The shift of attitude, perspective, and behavior that will heal our medical system is probably the same shift that will heal us all.

Sarah: *You've done something quite unconventional for a physician, which is to acknowledge uncertainty, mystery, not knowing the answers. What do you gain and lose with that sort of an approach?*

Rachel: Well, first of all, I'm a quite conventional physician, but I think what you're pointing to is something far deeper than medicine.

I was taught to deal with mystery as if it was a hemorrhage, to deal with the unknown as if it was an emergency. I now move towards mystery and the unknown rather than away from it, and in a culture focused on *mastery*, as ours is, that's unconventional. I don't think I've lost anything by doing that. Often it's a sense of mystery that provides strength in difficult times.

I do a lot of my work with a rather remarkable artist, Marian Weber. For her, the unknown is a blank canvas, and you don't quickly fill it with doodles and squiggles. You don't make up stories to fill the unknown like doctors do – stories like, "you have six months to live." You sit before the unknown, recognizing it for what it is, with patience, and you wait for revelation. I've learned to recognize that when somebody has a diagnosis, "You have cancer," this is a confrontation with the unknown.

I was told at the age of 15 that I would have multiple surgeries, and I'd be dead by the time I was 40. And I made a lot of life decisions based on that. I have had those multiple surgeries – I've had abdominal surgery seven times – and of course, I've been dead now for about 18 years! I think that by not presenting my diagnosis to me as an unknown, I lost a great deal in my life.

Sarah: *How do you think you would have lived your life differently?*

Rachel: I lost a great sense of possibility for my life, and for many years my dreams became constricted.

Sarah: *In your book, you talk about seeing the face of God in folded sheets. I love the idea that we can find meaning even in mundane tasks like housework!*

Rachel: It is a beautiful phrase. I think the sense of service implied in that is one of the deepest wisdoms: recognizing the sacred in the ordinary.

Putting a cup of soup in front of a six-year-old child is a statement of trust in the future and connection to life. Now you could also fling the soup down in front of the child and say, "Hurry. Eat this, so I can get that bowl into the dishwasher." There's a lot of choice in this, don't you think?

Many of us are afraid to go deep. When we feel empty, we just put more and more and more new and often superficial stuff in, so we still stay empty. The only way to fill yourself up is to go deep into what we already have, and very powerful things can happen then.

Sarah: *How do you maintain that depth of wisdom if you're caught up in work that feels like drudgery or always keeps you busy?*

Rachel: I have a wise friend named Angeles Arrien, and one of the things she teaches is the keeping of journals. At the end of the day you sit down for five minutes and answer three questions:

"What surprised me today?"

"What moved me or touched me today?"

"What inspired me today?"

I do this with doctors and medical students. On the first day he tried this, a surgeon in one of my programs wrote: "Nothing." "Nothing." "Nothing."

And the next day again: "Nothing." "Nothing." "Nothing."

He said he found it very irritating; he did not like to fail at things. And so he vowed to try a little harder, and he began to look around him with more wish to see. Later he told me, "Rachel, I was surrounded by heroes, and I didn't know it."

This changes everything. People are surprised eight or nine hours after something happens when they look back on it deliberately. But that gap shortens until eventually they are able to see in the *very moment* what surprises them, what touches them, and what inspires them. And then everything changes. The world has not changed, but they have begun to be able to *see* the world, and they can then communicate that experience.

You know, Sarah, it's a very powerful thing because someone will turn to a colleague and say, "I was inspired by the way you dealt with that. I was very touched by it. I thought they were very lucky to have you for a doctor." Or someone can say to a patient, "Mrs. Jones, I am endlessly surprised by your good will and your ability to carry on despite everything, and I find it very inspiring." It's a question of paying attention. There is a saying which goes, "The voyage of discovery lies not in seeking new vistas but in having new eyes."

Sarah: *That relates back to what you were saying earlier about listening.*

Rachel: Keeping a journal is a form of listening – learning to listen to life. Often healing is not becoming more than who we are, it's undoing the way we have fixed ourselves in order to win the approval of those around us. It's returning to our own integrity, even though the integrity may at first feel unfamiliar because we've never lived from there before. It's reclaiming the parts we've put in our shadow. And some of those parts may be very powerful and positive parts for which we could not get acceptance from the people around us. So it's more like an uncovering process, rather than an adding on of something new.

Sarah: *What advice would you give to someone who has a friend or a loved one who is very ill, or perhaps is dying?*

Rachel: The one thing I would say is to remember that your caring matters. Even though you may feel helpless to cure the person's illness, the fact that you care ultimately matters a great deal; it strengthens them to deal with what they have to deal with. When I was young and sick, I was a very angry person and I often pushed people away. But I felt their caring nonetheless, and the fact that they cared about my suffering is what, in the end, allowed me to reclaim myself.

So I think healing lies in relationship. It lies in reclaiming the web of connection, which is what sustains life. It lies in reclaiming the power and mystery in our relationships to each other and to this world. And healing relationships are mutual. I think most of us don't value our love enough in this culture. We value our expertise. But, our expertise will not make us whole and it will not make the world whole either. In the end, it's our love that matters.

Muhammad Yunus is the founder of the Grameen Bank, now the largest rural bank in Bangladesh and an internationally recognized model of micro-credit that caters to the poorest of the poor – and especially to women.

The End of Poverty

Investment and business can enhance creativity, conserve the environment, and even help end poverty. Hard to believe? Muhammad Yunus is showing how it's done.

Sarah van Gelder: *What was it that inspired you to begin a micro-credit program, and when did you realize that you were on to an important concept?*

Muhammad Yunus: I had been teaching in the United States, and I returned to Bangladesh after independence to participate in rebuilding the nation. I came with the arrogance of a Ph.D.; I thought we could solve the problems of Bangladesh. Once I was there, I was confronted with a nationwide famine, and the arrogance melted away. I felt humbled. I couldn't do anything.

Then I decided that, rather than worrying about what happens to the whole world, or Bangladesh, or the famine situation, I would just find out what I could do to help one person have a better day. I started going to people's houses, talking to them, trying to understand their lives. I saw how people suffered for lack of a tiny amount of money. One dollar, two dollars can make so much difference in a life. We made a list of 42 people who needed a total of only $27, less than one dollar apiece. That was the biggest shock. How can people suffer for want of such small sums of money? The government was allocating millions of dollars, yet nobody cared how people suffered for such a tiny amount.

My first response was to loan them money from my own pocket. Then I thought once I started, I would have to keep on lending my money. I should arrange with the bank to make the loans.

I approached a bank, but the bank manager said, "No, no, no. You cannot lend money to poor people. They will not pay you back."

"How do you know?" I asked. "Have you ever tried?"

"No, we don't have to. We know they don't."

I said, "We'll find out. I think they will pay it back."

It's a long story, but in the end I offered the bank my services as a guarantor. I borrowed the money from the bank, loaned it to the poor, and people paid it back.

But the bankers still said, "Oh, you're a fool. They will repay the money this time, but the moment you loan more, they'll stop." I was told that the loans were repaid because the borrowers were all from one village where I had been meeting and talking with the people. So I did it in two villages, then five, ten, twenty villages, thirty villages, a hundred villages. Each time it worked. Each time the bankers waited for the whole thing to collapse, and it did not. It grew.

Finally I decided to set up my own bank. The government thought it was a funny idea; poor people cannot borrow money. I showed them the examples, the reports, but they didn't pay any attention. I lobbied, knocking on doors for two years. Finally, I was given permission, and we became a bank.

Sarah: *From what I understand, the work you're doing leads to changes in people's lives that go beyond their immediate economic well-being. Can you talk a little bit about the changes you see?*

Muhammad: This work is not just about loaning money, paying it back, and hoping that things will change. We also engage the people who borrow from us in discussions about the social problems that they face in their lives and the kind of solutions they imagine for themselves.

Something we call "The 16 Decisions" emerged out of thousands and thousands of these sessions. For example, one of the 16 Decisions says, "We shall grow vegetables all year round, eat plenty of them, and sell the surplus."

A lot of children have night blindness due to vitamin A deficiency, and this decision helps to overcome malnutrition. Another one is, "We shall send our children to school so that they can become educated."

An especially important one is "We shall not take any dowry at the time of marriage of our sons, and we shall not give any dowry at the time of marriage of our daughters."

A dowry is a curse; it destroys family after family who have to find the money to arrange the marriage of a daughter. As a result, a daughter becomes a family liability. The moment she is born, the family looks upon the daughter as a kind of punishment. Throughout her life the daughter lives in a very apologetic way. "Sorry I was born to be a daughter. I wish I was not born." The only way to resolve this is for people to agree not to take dowries and not to give them.

Another one of the 16 Decisions is "We shall keep our families small, increase our income, and reduce our expenditures." Studies show that Grameen Bank families adopt family planning practices at twice the rate of the national average.

Sarah: *What other changes have grown out of the Grameen process? At your scale, do you believe you are making changes in the political arena?*

Muhammad: We had a national election in June. We had a tremendous voter turnout, 73 percent average nationwide. The fascinating thing was that for the first time in the history of Bangladesh, women voters turned out in larger numbers than male voters. One common explanation is that more women voted because organizations such as Grameen and other micro-credit groups have organized them. Women are attending weekly meetings and developing leadership and greater awareness. When the election came, women wanted to be sure their voices were heard.

In the process, the fundamentalist party, which had 17 seats in the previous Parliament, was completely wiped out. They won only three seats, because the women don't vote for them. The message was very clear – they were defeated everywhere.

These are the things that generate power and change consciousness. One thing leads to another. With money and empowerment, people start seeing themselves as people who can make decisions.

Sarah: *I understand that Grameen has moved into other areas beyond micro-lending. Could you tell me a little bit about that, and why you've chosen to do so?*

Muhammad: We have observed that while Grameen credit helps people increase their income, several leakages in the system keep people from moving ahead. One is the expenditures for health care. When you're extremely poor, you don't spend any money on your health because you are preoccupied with getting food. Once you satisfy that basic need, you start diverting your additional income to health issues, and you can't move ahead. So, we decided that Grameen should look into Bangladesh health care.

In Bangladesh, child mortality is extremely high, one of the highest in the world. Maternal death at delivery is also very high. There is no prenatal examination or postnatal treatment of the mother. The government organizes health services in Bangladesh, but does so very poorly. We decided to develop a modern, self-financing health care program that addresses the issues of the poor and emphasizes prevention.

For the last three years we have been operating an experimental Grameen health program at 10 different sites. Our plan was that the village borrowers would contribute to the program and help set it up. We found that for about two dollars a year per family, we could develop a very good health care program with modern facilities for an entire area. Currently, we can cover 65 percent of the cost. We are trying to get to the point where we recover 100 percent of our costs so that we can expand the program throughout the country.

Sarah: *Why were you able to do this when the government had such difficulty providing the services?*

Muhammad: Somehow, whenever the government is involved, corruption becomes an issue. The Bangladesh government spends a lot of money on health care, but the program is doctor-oriented. There are beautiful hospitals, clinics, and so forth, but people don't get health services. Doctors have a private practice somewhere else and come back at the end of the month to pick up the check. The government cannot change anything because the people in the programs are so powerful.

Sarah: *Your program won't run into the same difficulties when it grows?*

Muhammad: Our decision-making process is different – it is performance oriented. The government is oriented toward supporting its cronies and maintaining the status quo. They are not interested in the health results.

Another area is our hand-loom products. Bangladesh has more than a million families of hand-loom weavers – those who make fabrics. At one time, a Bangladeshi hand-loom product called muslin was the coveted fabric in the royal courts of Europe. When the European colonial powers came, machine-made fabrics came with them, and the colonial rulers forced the hand-loom industry nearly out of existence. It survives only to meet local needs, but now even the local hand-loom market is getting squeezed by imported machine-made fabric and by shiploads of very cheap used clothing.

So we thought we could help the weavers survive by expanding the export market for their fabric. We created Grameen Check, a good quality 100 percent cotton fabric, light on the body. In the first year, we didn't do so well, but this year we will easily exceed $10 million. Once the business is successful, we'll start selling shares to the weavers and they'll become the owners of the company. We created another company, Grameen Products to make and sell Bangladeshi shirts and saris.

Another project, the Grameen Social Venture Capital Fund, invests venture capital in businesses that have possibility but are too risky for anyone else. For example, a lot of Grameen borrowers buy cows and sell milk, but there are no good processing facilities in the country. If someone would build processing plants, we could process the milk and market it in areas that need it. The milk price would go up, and our borrowers would benefit.

We are also in the process of creating a mutual fund, a kind of retirement fund for our borrowers. Most families want to have a large number of children because they're unsure about their future. We believe their eagerness to have more children will diminish once they know that their old age is protected.

Then we got a license to operate a telephone company and created Grameen Phone. Most telephone companies in Bangladesh concentrate only in the cities. The telephone is a symbol of authority, and we want to break that image and bring cellular telephones to the poor women in the villages. We see this as a business proposition, but at the same time it has a social dimension. For example, one village woman could become the "telephone lady." Anybody who wants to make a call will come to her house, or invite her to their house. She could charge for the house-calls and makes it a business.

A telecommunication network could be extended all over the country, not just concentrated in the cities. Rural people could have access to market information. Having telephones will help women, because most of the abuse of women in villages happens because of the women's isolation. They can't tell anybody because they have no means to communicate to the outer world. If the telephone is introduced gradually into village life, we think useful changes will emerge. We hope that within the next six months we'll be operating from the villages in Bangladesh. In the next four or five years, we hope to be in place throughout the whole of Bangladesh.

Now that we have Grameen Phone, we decided to create Grameen Cybernet. Our aim is to bring Internet facilities to rural areas so that the whole world can be at their doorstep. They can get information and send information, and even start new businesses like data-entry or software development right in the villages.

Over the next 20 to 25 years the world will become a sort of borderless, distanceless place. The villages should not be excluded from that world. They should be integrated into it so that a village in Bangladesh and a city like Seattle are just next door to each other.

Sarah: *Do you have any concerns about the western culture of Hollywood and Madison Avenue, and all the values that go with it, coming in force into village life?*

Muhammad: Information is not a one-way flow. Of course, western culture has a lot more strength because it's more organized, it's marketable, and it comes on strong. But gradually, the other side will get organized and say, "We have a market too. You're interested in our music, our culture, our art, and our things." Lots of interchanges will take place, and a global kind of culture will emerge with, of course, local variations.

While we dream about the Internet and cellular telephones, we have to face the reality that 85 percent of the villages in Bangladesh don't have electricity, so we created another company called Grameen Energy. Conventional energy will never get to those villages, so we are seriously negotiating with solar companies around the world to bring in solar energy.

We are also considering electricity produced by biomass, gas, and wind power. Through the Grameen network, we can reach out to any village and find Grameen borrowers who can be the energy suppliers to the village, like the telephone lady. We can create micro-power supply companies.

Sarah: *I notice you're focusing on renewable energy sources that don't, for the most part, contribute to global warming.*

Muhammad: Yes, we worry about global warming. Our survival will depend on how the whole world community behaves, particularly the industrialized nations that contribute the most to global warming. If global warming raises the water level by a foot, a part of Bangladesh will be submerged – the land is very flat, just slightly above sea level.

We also know that *we* have to be careful about the environment because our survival depends on a sustainable environment. Our soil feeds 120 million people today. In the next 25 years, at the present rate, the population will probably double. Where will we find our food if we destroy our soil? We have to look critically at chemical use and consider organic ways, including returning biomass to our land. Insecticide is another concern because in the process of attacking pests, we also destroy the friendly creatures that help the soil and plants.

People must become very aware of what we do to our environment, because it is not going to get any bigger. How do we maintain energy supplies or the capacity of the soil to produce food for us 20 years from now, 50 years from now, so that we can still have a world that will sustain life?

Sarah: *The businesses you've described operate under different environmental and social principles than most business.*

Muhammad: Behind all of our projects is the idea that business doesn't have to be greed-based; it can be run with social objectives. For example, I am interested in making good health care available to all people in a businesslike way. My purpose is not to make myself rich.

Some might say "Oh, that may be true in the East, but there is nobody like that in the West." But people everywhere feel pleasure when they do something for a fellow human being. That pleasure is much more important than the one that comes from making tons of money and being on the list of billionaires. I want to feel that I'm useful to my neighbor, to my friend, and to somebody else. I want people to say, "You're a good man."

In any area – education, health, communication, fashion – you can achieve social objectives and still be in the marketplace and be competitive. I think that as more socially motivated people enter the marketplace, greedy people will begin to be squeezed out, because people will support those who are in business for the good of all.

We have to redesign the marketplace by attracting socially motivated people. A global network of such people could help provide the support to achieve these objectives. They can learn from each other to be innovative, creative, and to solve problems – problems of the inner city, the villages, the problem of poverty in the world.

Sarah: *You're really talking about the possibility of eliminating poverty.*

Muhammad: Yes, very much. I don't understand why anybody should be poor on this planet. There is more than enough to make everybody happy – not by giving things away, but by enhancing the capability of each person and by creating an enabling environment. There is enough inside each person to take care of himself or herself. Every person has the ability to create his or her own job. If society was structured for self-employment, there would be no reason to fear becoming poor. We worry because we look to those who are hiring rather than to ourselves. We really can create our own job, make money, and take care of ourselves.

The problem is we have built a society in which some are excluded from the marketplace. That's why I am critical about the financial institutions that bar large numbers of people around the world from entering the marketplace. Grameen is a mechanism for integrating people back into the marketplace. It opens up opportunities for people to build their own lives.

Sarah: *In your view, how is the situation different for the poor in industrialized countries, as opposed to the poor in Bangladesh?*

Muhammad: It is basically the same. It's a rejection by society. The poor do not create poverty. The institutions we build and the policies we pursue create poverty. If you want to cure the cause of poverty, you have to change the mind-set of the institutions. If we have this kind of change in the marketplace, a new civilization can be built. I see a world that is absolutely free from poverty. I'm not talking about a remote future, but in our lifetimes, perhaps the next 25, 30, or 40 years. It can happen.

Lysa Leland

Dr. Karl-Henrik Robèrt, a Swedish cancer doctor and medical researcher, founded The Natural Step to bring a solid scientific foundation into polarized environmental debates – and provide a framework for action.

The Natural Step: The Science of Sustainability

What does life require? Can an advanced, technological society sustain the conditions needed to support life on Earth? Here's a scientifically grounded framework that lays out our choices – and their consequences.

Sarah van Gelder: *How did you go from being a doctor to taking on this large question of sustainability?*

Karl-Henrik Robèrt: My career centered on my work as a medical doctor heading a cancer ward in a university hospital, the largest one outside of Stockholm. I was concerned with the environment as a private human being, but I didn't know what I could do except to pay my dues to Greenpeace and other NGOs.

My epiphany came one day when I was studying cells from cancer patients. It hit me that cells are the unifying unit of all living things. The differences between our cells and the cells of plants are so minor that it's almost embarrassing; the makeup is almost identical all the way down to the molecular level. You can't argue with them or negotiate with them. You can't ask them to do anything they can't do. And their complexity is just mind blowing! Since politicians and business people also are constituted of cells, I had a feeling that a broad understanding of these cells might help us reach a consensus on the basic requirements for the continuation of life.

Most people are not aware that it took living cells about 3.5 billion years to transform the virgin soup of the atmosphere – which was a toxic, chaotic mixture of sulfurous compounds, methane, carbon dioxide, and other substances – into the conditions that could support complex life.

In just the last *decades* humans have reversed this trend. First we found concentrated energy like fossil fuels and nuclear power. As a result, we can create such a high throughput of resources that natural processes no longer have the time to process the waste and build new resources. Dispersed junk is increasing in the system as we lose soils, forests, and species. So we have reversed evolution. The Earth is running back towards the chaotic state it came from at a tremendous speed.

On an intuitive level, everyone knows that the natural environment is also the habitat for our economy, and if it goes down the drain, so does the economy. Despite that, the green movement attacks business, and business reacts defensively. So much of the debate focuses on the details – so much is like monkeys chattering among the leaves of the tree while the trunk and roots die. I thought we could get beyond that stalemate if we could begin to build a consensus based on much more solid, comprehensive thinking.

Sarah: *What did you do with this insight? What was your plan for getting beyond the stalemate in the environmental debate?*

Karl: I had a daydream that I could write a consensus statement with other scientists about the conditions that are essential to life. Instead of asking them what environmental issues they disagreed on, I could ask them where there was agreement and use that as a basis for a consensus that would serve as a platform for sounder decision making in society.

In August 1988, when I wrote the first effort to frame a consensus, I believed that my colleagues would agree wholeheartedly with what I had written, since it was so well thought through! Actually, it took 21 iterations to reach a consensus among this group of 50 ecologists, chemists, physicists, and medical doctors.

I was able to raise funds to mail this consensus statement as a booklet with an audio cassette to all 4.3 million households in Sweden. This statement describes how badly we are performing with respect to the natural systems around us and how dangerous the situation is. It makes the point that debating about policy is not bad in itself – but it is bad when the debate is based on misunderstandings and poor knowledge. It doesn't matter if you are on the left or the right, the consensus platform takes us beyond arguments about what is and is not true. That was the start of The Natural Step.

Sarah: *Could you explain briefly the Natural Step system conditions?*

Karl: The four system conditions describe the principles that make a society sustainable. The first two system conditions have to do with avoiding concentrations of pollutants from synthetic substances and from substances mined or pumped from the Earth's crust to ensure that they aren't systematically increasing in nature. The third condition says we must avoid overharvesting and displacing natural systems. System condition number four

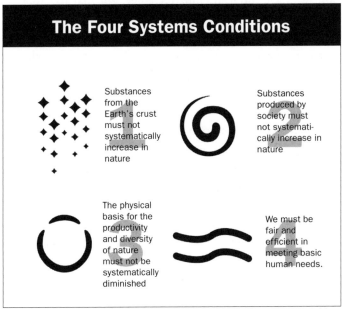

courtesy of The Natural Step

says we must be efficient when it comes to satisfying human needs by maximizing the benefit from the resources used.

Today, society is well outside the framework set by these conditions, and as a result, we are running towards increasing economic problems as we run out of fresh and non-polluted resources.

Sarah: So if we follow these conditions we can avoid the reverse evolution you mentioned earlier – we can quit dispersing persistent substances into the biosphere and make it possible for nature to continue to provide us with the basic resources we need to live – soil, air, a stable climate, water, and so on. In other words, these conditions will help us judge whether our actions are sustainable. Is this an approach that businesses and government officials find compelling?

Karl: I think most people in business understand that we are running into a funnel of declining resources globally. We will soon be 10 billion people on Earth – at the same time as we are running out of forests, crop land, and fisheries. We need more and more resource input for the same crop or timber yield. At the same time, pollution is increasing systematically, and we have induced climate change. All that together creates a resource funnel.

By decreasing your dependence on activities that violate the system conditions, you move towards the opening of the resource funnel. You can do this through step by step reducing your dependence on:

• heavy metals and fossil fuels that dissipate into the environment (condition #1)

• persistent unnatural compounds like bromine-organic anti-flammables or persistent pesticides (condition #2)

• wood and food from ecologically maltreated land and materials that require long-distance transportation (condition #3)

• wasting resources (system #4).

Any organization that directs its investments towards the opening of the funnel through complying with these system conditions will do better in business than its ignorant competitors. This is due to inevitable changes at the wall of the funnel in the form of increased costs for resources, waste management, insurance, loans, international business agreements, taxes, and public fear.

In addition, there is the competition from those who direct their investments more skillfully towards the opening of the funnel – thus avoiding those costs – and sooner or later get rewarded by their customers.

Once we understand the funnel, the rest is a matter of timing, and time is now running out. Many corporations have already run into the wall of the funnel as a result of violating the system conditions. And today many companies are getting relatively stronger in comparison with others as a result of previous investments in line with the system conditions. Of course there are a large number of companies who still benefit in the short term from violating the principles of the common good, but in the long run, they have no future.

So if you ask business people, "Do you think that this could possibly influence tomorrow's market?" they get embarrassed, because they all understand it will. The issue is to foresee the nature of that influence, because if you do, you will prosper from it

Sarah: *I want to ask you about the fourth condition, because that's the one that has been most controversial, perhaps because it is based on human systems more than natural systems.*

Karl: The fourth principle is about the internal resource flows in a society, but it is still a logical first-order principle that follows as a conclusion from the first three. The reason people regard the fourth principle as a separate value is the word "fairness," which is part of the fourth principle.

Most people understand that the first three principles set a frame for societal behavior. If matter from the Earth's crust is no longer going to systematically increase in concentration, nor man-made compounds, and if we are going to live from the interest of what nature gives us – not use up nature's capital – the first-order conclusion is that we must be much more efficient about how we meet our needs.

Fairness is an efficiency parameter if we look at the whole global civilization. It is not an efficient way of meeting human needs if one billion people starve while another billion have excess. It would be more efficient to distribute resources so that at least vital needs were met everywhere. Otherwise, for example, if kids are starving somewhere, dad goes out to slash and burn the rain forest to feed them – and so would I if my kids were dying. And this kind of destruction is everyone's problem, because we all live in the same ecosphere.

Sarah: *I realize you reached a consensus among Sweden's scientists on these foundational questions, but has your approach been controversial in the larger society?*

Karl: No. The business community found it refreshing to be involved in a dialogue that did not involve someone pointing fingers at them and telling them what they should do. This dialogue was the opposite of that; it involved a group of scientists describing the situation with regards to the environment and then asking for advice about how to remove the obstacles to sustainability. The business community, municipalities, and farmers actually enjoyed being part of it.

Sarah: *Why do companies choose to adopt The Natural Step? Is it that they understand the science and want to contribute to a more sustainable world? Or do they see TNS primarily as a winning business strategy?*

Karl: It is a mixture of both, and it is hard to evaluate which is most important. My feeling is that top people in business have a tough image that they display in board rooms. Privately, after the board meeting, they would much rather do well by doing good, than do well by contributing to the destruction of our habitat. Because of the rational economic and strategic thinking of the system conditions, they can endorse TNS principles without losing face in front of their tough peers. But as time goes on, the "soft" values become more and more important.

Sarah: *In the research I've done on Green Plans in the Netherlands, I found that Dutch businesses were concerned that they would be less competitive if they held to higher environmental standards than businesses from other countries. How have you dealt with the issue of competitiveness in The Natural Step?*

Karl: If you look at the countries where business is very successful, it is not the countries where the standards are low. It is the countries that have set high goals for what they want to achieve. In the long run, you get competitiveness from *increasing* standards.

Sarah: *Can you give me some examples of some things in Sweden that have been done differently as a result of this understanding?*

Karl: The Natural Step introduces a shared mental model that is intellectually strict but simple to understand. These are the rules of sustainability; you can plug them into decision making about any product. The first thing that happens is that this stimulates creativity, because people enter a much smarter dialogue if they have a shared framework for their goals. We have written books of case studies about how people together found smart and flexible solutions to problems that seemed impossible to solve, including new products, logistics, suppliers, energy sources, and fuels. A strict shared mental model can really get people working together.

Sarah: *You mentioned that this approach requires thinking beyond the short term, and yet especially in the US, most CEOs are rewarded based on this quarter's profits, not on how well they are positioning the company for the decades to come. How can companies in that kind of setting take on this sustainability challenge?*

Karl: If you are audited at quarterly intervals and you can be sued for failing to earn the last buck possible, it is more difficult. But you can still develop a future scenario for your company in which it meets principles that make it ecologically, socially, and economically sustainable – because it is not *economically* sustainable to rely on behaviors that have no future.

Once you've developed that scenario, you look back from this imagined future and ask yourself how those sustainability principles might have been met and what you might do today to get there. The strategy for business is to select as the first steps toward sustainability those that fulfill two criteria: they must be flexible to build on in the future, and they must provide a return on investments relatively soon – like, for instance, an attractive car that can run on renewable energy as well as gasoline.

Sarah: *What do you see as the trends for the coming years in terms of a switch to more sustainable practices?*

Karl: A deepening intellectual understanding is a good starting point for change of values. Today, it is considered "rational" to think about economic growth only, whereas a focus on the underlying reason that people live to-gether in societies is considered non-rational. The TNS approach demonstrates that their present paradigm is, in fact, irrational and that we need new economic tools.

My belief is that free will of individuals and firms will not be sufficient to make sustainable practices widespread – legislation is a crucial part of the walls of the funnel, particularly if we want to make the transition in time.

But this is a dynamic process. The more examples we get of businesses entering the transition out of free will, the easier it will be for proactive politicians. In a democracy, there must be a "market" for proactive decisions in politics, and that market can be created by proactive businesses in dialogue with proactive customers. For example, in Sweden, some of these proactive business leaders are lobbying for green taxes. In that triangle of dialogue – business-market-politicians – a new culture may evolve, with an endorsement of the values we share but have forgotten how to pay attention to.

So, the flow goes: intellectual understanding, some practice and experience, deeper understanding with some change in attitude, prepared-ness for even more radical change, some more experience, even deeper under-standing, and eventually, an endorsement of the value systems that are inher-ent in the human constitution.

Sarah: *What worries you the most about the future? You have said that you anticipate some very difficult times for the world in the years ahead – perhaps even a collapse. Could you explain what you meant and what you think might cause such a collapse?*

Karl: What worries me the most is the systematic social battering of people all around the world, leading to more and more desperate people who don't feel any partnership with society because of alienation, poverty, dissolving cultural structures, more and more "molecular" violence (unorganized and self-destructive violence that pops up everywhere without any meaning at all). The response of the establishment is superficial, with more and more imprisonment and money spent on defense against those feared, leading to a vicious cycle.

If this goes on long enough, a constructive and new sustainable paradigm among governments and business leaders will not necessarily help us in time. We will have more and more people who are so hungry to meet their vital human needs that it will be hard to reach them.

Sarah: *What keeps you energized in the face of these enormous challenges? What are your sources of hope?*

Karl: My vision is that we develop a mainstream understanding that nobody wins from destroying our habitat and that you do better in business if you work as though society will become sustainable and as though different cultures will survive, because cultural diversity is also essential.

To maintain hope, we cannot focus only on the dark things that are going on. Once in a while if you get a "bird's eye" perspective, you see all sorts of good examples, and they comfort you. You see more and more people who understand and who are making concrete contributions to the transition to this new understanding.

Catherine Allport

The Great Turning

Joanna Macy is a scholar of Buddhism and of general systems theory and author of *Coming Back to Life, World as Lover, World as Self,* and her new memoir entitled, *Widening Circles*. This interview took place during the WTO protests in Seattle.

Our changing experience of the Divine, our efforts to rein in a doomed economic system, and the emergence of new structures and ways of life – Joanna Macy weaves together possibilities for this unique time in human history.

Sarah van Gelder: We've been focused on the activities surrounding the World Trade Organization meeting here in Seattle for the last few days. As we speak, people are being arrested for walking in "no-protest" zones and bused off to jail. Before we head back into downtown ourselves, I want to ask for your reflections on change at a larger level, what you're calling "the Great Turning."

Joanna Macy: The term "Great Turning" is just one way to name the vast revolution that's going on because our way of life cannot be sustained. There are three main dimensions of it that I see.

The first involves holding actions that slow the destruction caused by the industrial growth society. This economic system is doomed because it measures its success by how fast it uses up the living body of Earth – extracting resources beyond Earth's capacity to renew, and spewing out wastes faster than Earth's capacity to absorb. It is now in runaway mode, devouring itself at an accelerating rate.

Holding actions are important because they buy time. They are like a first line of defense; they can save a few species, a few ecosystems, and some of the gene pool for future generations. In Seattle this week we saw how holding actions – in this case nonviolent blockades – can slow down efforts to give transnational corporations a yet freer hand in plundering our heritage.

But holding actions are not enough to create a sustainable society. You've got to have new social and economic structures, new ways of doing things. And these seem to be springing up at a faster rate than at any time in our human history. I consider *YES!* magazine so important precisely because you are pointing to these innovations, which are rarely reported in the mainstream, corporate-controlled media.

Alternative structures and analyses constitute the second dimension of the Great Turning. They were sure evident in all the teach-ins and resource sharing going on this week in Seattle. People are wising up to the assumptions and agreements that allow a few to get richer and richer while more and more people sink below the poverty line. Fresh social and economic experiments are sprouting, and new alliances are forming too. Yesterday I marched alongside farm workers and longshoremen, and I was moved to see how labor unions and environmental groups are making common cause at last.

But new coalitions and new ways of production and distribution are not enough for the Great Turning. They will shrivel and die unless they are rooted in deeply held values – in our sense of who we are, who we want to be, and how we relate to each other and the living body of Earth. That amounts to a shift in consciousness, which is actually happening now at a rapid rate. This is the third dimension of the Great Turning, and it is, at root, a spiritual revolution, awakening perceptions and values that are both very new and very ancient, linking back to rivers of ancestral wisdom.

I loved the banners and banter of yesterday's marchers, how they conveyed these values with such exuberance and humor, making fun of our greed and shortsightedness, and celebrating solidarity with all life from sea turtles to butterflies. The ancestors were in our midst, too; every block or two, a United Farm Workers' group with drums and feathers stopped to perform an Aztec dance.

Of course, a consciousness shift by itself is insufficient for the Great Turning; you also have to have the holding actions and the creation of alternative structures. These three dimensions are totally interdependent and mutually reinforcing. I love seeing it this way because it gets us off that dead argument: "Is it more important to work on yourself? or Is it more important to be out there on the barricades?" Those are such stupid arguments, because actually we have to do it all. And as we do it together, it gains momentum and becomes more self-sustaining.

You know, I often imagine that future generations will look back at us and say, "Oh, bless 'em. Those ancestors were right there in the Great Turning! There was so much they had to change, and they didn't even know if they could pull it off."

And we might not pull it off. There's no guarantee that this tremendous shift will kick in before our life support systems unravel irretrievably. Actually, the very fact that there's no guarantee of success is what will draw forth our greatest courage and creativity. If I could give you a pill or potion to convince you that everything is going to be okay, that would hardly elicit your purest creativity and chutzpah.

We could wait around forever before we act, trying to compute our chances of success. But our time to come alive is right now, on this edge of possibility.

From our own life experience, we know there's never a guarantee – whether we're falling in love, or going into labor to birth a baby, or devoting ourselves to a piece of land, turning the soil and watching for rain. We don't ask for proof that we'll succeed and that everything will turn out as we want. We just go ahead, because life wants to live through us!

Sarah: *In social movements of the past, it seems to me that people looked to a leader or to some doctrine to lead them forward. Now, people seem to take the responsibility upon themselves; they seem to want to know in their bones what needs to be done and how they can, authentically, be a part of it.*

Joanna: Yes. Everywhere I go, talking with folks of all ages and walks of life, I sense this search for authenticity. People are wanting to take responsibility for their lives, both politically and spiritually. It's beautiful.

At the most fundamental level, there's an appetite for reconnecting with the sacred. Instead of depending on anyone else for that connection, we want to be able to know it and embody it ourselves. What is the sacred? It's the ground of our being. It's the whole of which we are a part. It's what imbues our life with meaning and beauty. Of course, there are different ways of perceiving our relation to it. Mainstream western society has, by and large, related to the sacred by projecting it outwards, setting it apart as a God "out there" to worship and obey. We made the sacred transcendent, and in its honor created ziggurats, cathedrals, masterpieces of art and choral music – perhaps our greatest cultural achievements.

But after several millennia of assigning the sacred to a transcendent dimension removed from ordinary life, the world around us begins to go dead and loses its luminosity and meaning. The Earth is reduced to a supply store of material resources and a sewer for our wastes. And in such a world, devoid of the sacred, anything goes – buy up, sell off, consume as much as you can!

What's so beautiful about being alive at this moment is that the pendulum is starting to swing the other way. We are retrieving the projection. We are taking the sacred back into our lives. The swing is from transcendence to immanence. The most vital movement of our era involves making the sacred immanent again. I see it happening in every spiritual tradition – in the Jewish Renewal movement, in Creation Spirituality, in women's spirituality, and in the resurgence of Wicca, and the teachings of ancient indigenous peoples. We are reawakening to the sacredness of life itself, in the soil and air and water, in our brothers and sisters of other species, and in our own bodies.

I spoke of this as a swing of the pendulum, but a metaphor I like even better comes from Ludwig Feuerbach, a German theologian of the mid-19th century. He said that our apprehensions of the sacred have a rhythm like the pumping action of the heart. Just as the heart pumps blood out from the center of the body, we project outwards our sense of the sacred, so that we can behold its majesty and fall on our knees before it in wonder and awe. Feuerbach reminded us that the heartbeat is a two-way action – systole and diastole: the pumping out is followed by drawing the blood back through the heart. When the sacred becomes too remote, you take it back in, to let it lubricate your life. The retrieval of the projection is not an endpoint either. When we get stuck too long in immanence, the sacred becomes indistinguishable from anything else; it becomes bland, taken for granted. So the heartbeat goes on, ever renewing our sense of the holy. To perceive it this way frees me to see that they need each other, these two movements of the heart.

Sarah: *Tell me a little more about how it affects someone to start seeing the sacred as more immanent.*

Joanna: To see all life as holy rescues us from loneliness and the sense of futility that comes with isolation. The sacred becomes part of this encounter – part of you sitting in front of me, present in that stand of bamboo, and even in myself. I don't have to go to the Chartres cathedral to be in the presence of the Divine. It's right here.

This means that our sorrow is sacred, too. Within us all is grief for what is happening to our world – the despoiling of Earth, the extinction of our brother/sister species, the massive suffering of our fellow humans. But when we feel isolated, we stifle that sorrow and rage in order to fit in better and to avoid aggravating the loneliness.

Experiencing the sacred as immanent helps people to befriend their pain for the world and not fear that it will further isolate them. This is a matter of practical urgency, because to repress and discount the grief and dread we feel on behalf of all beings locks us into the status quo. In the work I do with groups, we reframe our pain for the world, recognizing it as the capacity to "suffer with," which is the literal meaning of compassion. It is not only honored in all spiritual traditions, it also serves as wholesome feedback, necessary to our survival. To recognize this brings us back to life: "It's okay for me to be here. It's okay for me to hurt, even. It's okay for me to weep for people who aren't even born yet. That's because I belong. That's because I am part of the sacred living body of Earth through all time."

This sense of belonging is spreading with the "new story" of our universe that Thomas Berry, Brian Swimme, Sister Miriam McGillis, and others are bringing in now. Drawing from the latest discoveries of science, they show how each of us is an inseparable part of this ever-unfolding story since it first began in the primal "flaring forth."

Everywhere I see people starting prayer groups and healing groups, sacred circles and home churches. They don't wait until they have Masters of Divinity degrees or are ordained. They're ordaining themselves. They are gathering together because they find they can experience this sacredness better in groups.

Moreover, people are expressing this sense of belonging by stepping forth. That was obvious in yesterday's march. People came in the scores of thousands because their hearts' desire now is for more than just drawing a paycheck so they can pay the mortgage and sit in front of the TV. They want to be out there with their fellow citizens, taking risks for the sake of something greater than their separate, individual lives.

When you act on behalf of something greater than yourself, you begin to feel it acting through you with a power that is greater than your own. The religious term for this empowerment is grace, and we conceived of it as coming from God. Now, we are feeling graced by other beings and by Earth itself. Those with whom and on whose behalf we act give us strength and eloquence and staying power we didn't know we had.

We celebrate this, for example, in the Council of All Beings. In that reverent and playful community ritual, we step aside from our human identity to speak on behalf of other life-forms. As the beings report the suffering they now experience, it becomes clear that their fate depends on that very species that is behaving with such greed and fear. So they decide to offer to the humans their own particular strengths. Whether you speak for eagle or worm or cypress tree, you think of what gifts you could share – farseeing eye, patience, readiness to go through the dark. In the process we realize that the gifts we're naming are already known to us and available. We just need to practice knowing that and remembering that we are sustained by each other in the web of life. Such practice helps us to decondition ourselves from centuries of old-paradigm thinking, which we've used in ways that have made us so lonely and selfish and nuts and powerless. It all goes together. Greed and powerlessness go together.

So we practice knowing our true power, which comes as a gift, like grace, because in truth it is sustained by others. We can draw on the wisdom and beauty and strengths of our fellow humans and our fellow species like so much money in the bank. I find that incredibly empowering, because it means I can go into a situation and trust that the courage and intelligence required will be supplied.

Sarah: *Let's circle back, now. How does this shift toward experiencing the Divine as immanent relate to the Great Turning you spoke of earlier?*

Joanna: I think the felt presence of the sacred will be like fuel for the Great Turning. It will help us hang in there through a tough time. In the breakdown of the Industrial Growth Society, things will get a lot harder and scarier for a while. And when we get scared we get mean. We turn on each other. I think our greatest danger is fear and the blaming and scapegoating that fear arouses. To hold the conviction that all life is holy will help us withstand the temptations to demagoguery and divisiveness.

Sarah: So what you're saying implies a different way of treating those whom we consider our opponents?

Joanna: Yes, yes. There's no private salvation in this. The people who don't agree with us become like a noble adversary, challenging us to develop our smarts and courage. We still have to walk together into the future. They're like brother/sister cells in the larger body of life. We may have to take some pretty strong, surgical steps to limit their exercise of greed, hatred, and stupidity. But those three poisons, as they're known in Buddhism, are the problem. We want to liberate our adversaries and ourselves from these three. We're not really free until they're free too. I think that helps with the exercise of nonviolence, don't you?

Sarah: Yes. It's such a tricky business because it can be very difficult to say, for example, "There's a real problem with corporate globalization. There's a real problem with the WTO." And at the same time recognize that the individuals who are involved in those activities are nonetheless as sacred as any other beings.

Joanna: And that they're in bondage to our real enemies, which are greed, hatred, and delusion. Delusion or ignorance means the notion that we are separate, that we can be immune to what we do to other people. Remember at the march yesterday, there was a tall figure on stilts dressed as the fat industrialist? I laughed and booed with the rest. I think it's great to make fun of Greed – so long as we don't demonize individuals who are caught up in its claws. I admit, it does get hard to avoid making people like Charles Hurwitz the target of my rage, and to remember, as Gandhi asked us to, that our target is not the person but their actions – the clearcutting of the redwoods, the lockouts of the steelworkers.

Sarah: One of the major sources of conflict around the world is differences in ethnicity, culture, and religion. If this sense of the Divine becoming immanent, if that is happening across religious traditions, could that be a sign of hope for conflicts among religions?

Joanna: Mmm. My mind flies to Afghanistan and the resurgence of a totalitarian patriarchy where the sacred is seen as punitive. Yet, out of the same religion comes Rumi and Hafiz and the Sufi tradition with its celebration of the sacredness of all life.

Fundamentalism rears its head in all religions now. It's a reaction against the radical uncertainty of this moment in history. In such times, we tend to revert to the security of rock-bound belief and vent our anxieties in scapegoating others. The temptation to take refuge in our own self-righteousness is strong.

But now there's also a strong current in the other direction. Last June, when my husband, Fran, and I were in Israel – that land so epochally torn by competing claims to the sacred – what we heard most of all from the Jews and the Arabs was their spiritual hunger to reconnect with each other. Clearly those to whom the sacred is becoming immanent have a role to play in easing the hatreds bred by the fundamentalists. And they are playing that role already.

People are sick and tired of being pitted against each other when there's already so much suffering and the Earth itself is under assault. They're ready to reconnect and honor the life we share. That is the great adventure of our time. And it's happening.

Additional copies of
Saying yes! are available
from the Positive Futures
Network for $7.50 plus
$2.50 for shipping and
handling.

Subscribe to *YES!* Magazine

YES! brings you stories of new ways of life that foster
community, are in harmony with Earth's ecosystems, and
build on the best of what it means to be human.

YES! Subscriptions — **$24/year**
(Canada add $5/year, other non-U.S. add $7 postage)
Please send your payment in U.S. funds payable to:

YES! A Journal of Positive Futures
PO Box 10818, Bainbridge Island, WA 98110-0818 USA
Phone: 206/842-0216 fax: 206/842-5208
Subscribe online at: www.yesmagazine.org
Or call toll free at 800/937-4451.